Notes from the Underwire

Notes from the Underwire

ADVENTURES
FROM MY AWKWARD
and LOVELY LIFE

Quinn
Cummings

HYPERION
New York

A million little adventures: These are the stories to the best of my recollection. It must be noted, however, that I've had five, maybe six concussions. So if any details are wrong, blame my intermittently swollen brain. I do know, however, that Alice is not my daughter's real name. I've changed it in these essays, because it's hard enough for her to have me as a mother.

Library of Congress Cataloging-in-Publication Data

Cummings, Quinn.
    Notes from the underwire : adventures from my awkward and lovely life / Quinn Cummings.
        p. cm.
    ISBN 978-1-4013-2286-1
    1. Cummings, Quinn.   2. Television actors and actresses—United States—Biography.   I. Title.
    PN2287.C694C86 2009
    791.4502'8092—dc22
    [B]   2008055376

Hyperion books are available for special promotions and premiums. For details contact the HarperCollins Special Markets Department in the New York office at 212-207-7528, fax 212-207-7222, or e-mail spsales@harpercollins.com.

Design by Karen Minster

FIRST EDITION

10 9 8 7 6 5 4 3 2 1

To Consort, for getting on the plane

ACKNOWLEDGMENTS

Thanks to Brenda Copeland for finding me in the wilderness. Thanks to Jeff Kleinman for support and counsel once I came in from the wilderness. Thanks to Mary Herczog, Ken Miller, and Jeff Greenstein for their wisdom and their mystifying belief that I was actually going to live through writing this. Thanks to Victoria Stafford and Michele East for their friendship and for each saying those unrepayable words, "When can I take your kid so you can write?" Thanks to everyone else I care about; I'd offer to bake you something as a thanks, but you all know what a dreadful cook I am.

Finally, thanks to my blog readers; your support and enthusiasm mean the world to me.

CONTENTS

Notes from the Underwire

My Original Nose

THIS WASN'T IN MY PLANS FOR THE DAY.

Alice and I attended a parent-and-child art class. While Alice mused over a composition that would be listed in future catalogs of her work as *Meditations on Pink Tissue, Elmer's Glue, and Glitter, #186,* I had taken a moment to run to the bathroom. Racing back so I could be the restraining force between Alice and a Big Gulp–sized container of glitter, I dashed up the stairs and bounded through the doorway into the classroom. Only, to keep things lively, I didn't pass through the open door but slammed into its adjacent plate-glass window instead. The flat light shining through from the classroom had rendered it invisible. Now it was abundantly visible thanks to the smeary marks made by my nose, lips, and cheek crashing into its surface at full trot.

This won't come as a shock to anyone who knows me. I started walking at nine months. I started walking into things at nine months and one hour. My everyday walk resembles the frantic dart of a small, excitable lizard, and I seem to be unable to grasp the notion that inanimate objects don't know how to get out of my way. Smashing into a window was a new trick altogether. I had mutated from lizard to sparrow.

The door opened—the real door, not the portal of shame—and several parents and the art instructor looked at me with concern. The sound of my face slamming against the thick glass

must have been somewhat alarming. One of the parents, a casually well-dressed dad in his forties, came to where I was sitting
on the linoleum and asked, "Are you all right?"

I thought about this question. Noses were not designed to
absorb the impact from a head-to-wall collision at any speed
above a crawl so the odds of my being fully all right weren't good.
I thought about this for some time. Perhaps too much time. I
wondered if I had a concussion. Surreptitiously, I held out two
fingers and counted them. This cheered me up until I realized
someone else was supposed to run that test. If I'm holding up
two fingers there's a pretty high likelihood I'll know I'm holding
up two fingers. Unless, of course, the concussion is affecting my
memory, in which case I might be able to recognize two fingers
but wonder whose nail-nibbled fingers they are, which would
be another problem. Since the recollection of smooshing my
face into plate glass was excruciatingly vivid, I had every reason
to suspect my memory was unaffected. None of these thoughts
helped answer the immediate question regarding my health,
however, so I went with the always classic, "Yes, I'm fine."

As the concerned father stared deeply into my eyes, I worried for a moment that he found idiots who think they can pass
through solid objects desirable and was about to hit on me.
Then I noticed his gaze had a certain professional quality.

"Are you a doctor?" I asked, discreetly dabbing under my
eyes to see if my brain was leaking out.

"I was a cardiac surgeon. Now I run a medical-research hedge
fund."

Ladies and gentlemen, may I present the most intimidating
father in this area code, talking to the woman who had just seen
fit to emulate a windshield gnat. I dabbed. I smiled. I assured

everyone that I was fine. Really. Fine! Eventually, we all returned to our art making.

Dr. Hedge-Fund and his son went back to creating Michelangelo's *David* out of cotton balls and paste while they parried some sort of word game in Mandarin. I slid into the seat next to Alice where her work surface, her lap, and her hair led me to understand she had moved into the glitter phase of her creation without my counsel. She looked up. "Weren't you going to the bathroom?" When a small girl is struck by glitter-lust, her mother can leave the room, fling herself loudly against a solid object, and rest easy in the knowledge she wasn't missed.

I spent the better part of that night in front of the bathroom mirror poking at my nose, flinching, and poking it some more. Under the best of circumstances I am no great fan of my nose. For one thing, its bridge is too flat. For another, it's too short, and the combination of wide and short means my nose looks square, an adjective never associated with the great beauties of any era. It's a tolerable nose in person but it never photographs well. From certain angles it looks like I have a potato taped to my face. After the window incident, I appeared to have sprung a butcher-block workbench between my eyes. I was starting to miss the familiar square.

To add further insult to my injury, my nose was no longer drawing in the usual amounts of air. My left nostril had closed up shop and taken to its bed. I wanted to whine and I needed to find someone obligated to feign interest in all this. So, of course, I buttonholed Consort.

"Why did every self-defense course I've ever taken tell me how easy it is to break a person's nose?" I asked him.

Consort stared at me expectantly. I sighed, and a few moments passed.

He said, "That was rhetorical, right?"

"It seems so unfair," I continued, ignoring his question. "I was always told the nose breaks easily. I should be in pre-op for a nose job right now."

He stared at me in wonder and confusion. "I'm sorry, am I hearing you say you want a nose job?"

"Of course, I want a nose job. I hate my nose. It should be cuter. Or it should at least deliver oxygen to my brain. A nose job might accomplish one of those requirements."

"Then . . ." he said softly, tiptoeing through the minefield that is my belief system, "you should get a nose job . . ."

"You silly. I can't do that," I said patiently. "That would be cheating."

I will explain. When you live in Los Angeles your entire life, it's drummed into you how nothing is permanent. Don't like your name? Change it. "Tawnee" is nice, and isn't in high rotation this season. Breasts can expand and contract with the style of the moment. A chin-length bob can become tumbling locks in an afternoon and pixie-short by nightfall. The official motto of Los Angeles is "Semper Pulcher et Connubialis." Loosely translated, this means: "You are entitled by sheer virtue of being born to remain ever young and sexually desirable. You also get to possess any object that delights you."

Since every person in Los Angeles with a working credit card and a phone is currently interviewing plastic surgeons to redo their liposuction or freshen up their labia, I must—as the most contrary person in the world—get *nothing* changed. I must live with the nonphotogenic, nonfunctional nose I was given because living with the nose I was given at birth is making a point, even if I no longer recall what that point is.

My attitude might have had something to do with being honest. Or seeking a stoic calm. Or not wanting a nose that screams "Dr. Feingold's Spring 2008 collection." Still, as I explained to Consort, even the best laws have loopholes. I can get a face-lift when I'm older because a face-lift wouldn't actually change anything, it would just restore me to a previous condition—a condition I might have kept had I been more vigilant about sunblock, eaten nothing but cruciferous vegetables, and lived in a gravity-free environment. A face-lift isn't cheating; it doesn't change what I was given by nature. A face-lift is just a horrendously expensive do-over, with Vicodin.

Consort, as he often does after I explain how things work, attempted to present a neutral expression. But he just looked alarmed.

The next morning, my nose was blue. Not navy blue, more of an aquamarine. Certainly nothing I couldn't hide with a little makeup, but since touching my nose sent waves of pain down to my floating ribs, I was just going to have to dress around it. For entertainment value, I called my ear-nose-and-throat doctor. It was before 9:00 a.m. so his service asked if I wanted to leave a message.

"Yeah, just let him know that I ran into a plate-glass window yesterday and my nose didn't bleed or anything but now it's sort of aquamarine-blue and I can't breathe through one nostril, and also, I don't want to sound shallow, but I'm a little asymmetrical, I mean, we're all asymmetrical, right, but this is . . ."

"Please hold."

I assumed she had another call. I tried humming along to the hold music, but humming made my nose vibrate unpleasantly so I stopped. Within a minute, I heard my doctor's voice.

"Quinn," he said jovially. "What did you do now?"

I will never use my ENT doctor as a character witness; he knows too much. He always sees me at my worst, which frequently involves Q-tips and an eardrum. At least this was a new injury. I suspect he likes me in the same way police officers maintain an amicable rapport with certain neighborhood criminals. Everyone has their job, nothing personal. Three or four times a year I put my health at risk. Three or four times a year he comes along and saves me from myself, always taking care to laugh at my misadventures in the least derisive way possible. He'd see me that afternoon.

I took my Easter egg–tinted nose to Beverly Hills, where all doctors in Los Angeles practice. To outsiders, Beverly Hills is where celebrities congregate on corners, comparing Bentleys. In reality, Beverly Hills is where celebrities wear paper kimonos, read last month's *Good Housekeeping*, and urinate in a cup. The nurse called my name and pointed down the hallway. "You're in room seven," she said.

This was only slightly helpful as none of the doors displayed any sort of number. I drifted toward the first room and the nurse called out, "Not six. Seven!" in a tone that indicated even coliform bacteria knew how to find room seven. Stung, I spun around and followed her finger toward the next door, moving quickly to get away from her judgment and my disgrace. As it turns out, this was room five. Rooms seven and five were identical except the door into room seven was open and the door into room five was closed. I had run into another closed door.

It's not that I never learn. I learn things all the time. The lesson I'm learning now is that learning things doesn't change my behavior. When I was sixteen, I started saying "I don't actually like acting . . ." but it took another eight years for me to finish the sentence, "and I'm not going to do it anymore." Since I was eleven I've known I can't wear yellow, but every three years I convince myself "butter" or "lemon drop" isn't really yellow and I wear it until a close friend inquires if I might be experiencing liver failure. By the time I was twenty-four, I was already exquisitely aware that nothing good ever happened after the phrase, "Yes, let's get another pitcher of margaritas," but I continued that behavior for years. It's like one part of my brain takes notes and learns but the rest of my brain shouts "LA LA LA. Can't possibly hear you over this questionable activity." I sometimes wonder if my last words on this earth will be something like, "Oh, I *knew* this wouldn't work."

I was sitting on the floor in front of the examining room. The nurse who had been directing me into room seven raced over to me, saying, "Oh my God, are you okay?" which would have sounded better had she not been giggling and I not flat on my ass on the linoleum. I dabbed at my nose with a professional air and said briskly, "Just getting my money's worth out of today's visit." I stood up, looked around carefully, and determined the only other room with an open door must be room seven. I had every intention of walking in a steady and measured pace into the room. Instead, I darted across the hallway, hit my elbow on the counter, and flung myself into the chair in the examination room, prepared to be mocked yet again by my favorite doctor.

It hurts when I bang into things . . . I thought to myself, rubbing the bruise forming on my leg. If there was a second part to that sentence, it didn't come to me.

If It Weren't for the Vegetables

I LOVE GOING TO THE LOCAL FARMERS' MARKET; I'M SO much cooler there. For two hours a week I'm not the Quinn who would live on jelly beans if gum disease and diabetes didn't exist. I'm not the Quinn who sneers at root vegetables, the Quinn who is frightened by leeks. Walking up and down the rows of stands, I become the Quinn who spontaneously whips up a spinach salad with homemade vinaigrette for lunch, the one who buys vegetables and not only eats them but makes stock from the remnants. I am sober and industrious and thrifty. I am Amish with the option of Velcro. That the farmers' market Quinn doesn't actually exist is a small irritant, sand on my psychic spinach.

A while ago, I took Alice to the market. Along with the masses of vegetables and fruits, there were small restaurant booths and vendors selling premade goods. I was holding up a bunch of Swiss chard trying to make myself believe I would actually cook it before it became slime when Alice suddenly breathed, "Ooh, look." I followed her gaze to where a local Indian restaurant was selling takeout from an ice chest. Since we both appreciate a well-seasoned lentil, we ambled over. The setup was clean. The samples were generous and tasty. Predictably, I bought cooked lentils. And then Alice pointed to a pint-size container of something white.

"Yes! Raita!" she crowed, pleased at seeing her favorite exotic side dish. The owner gave her a small taste and she inhaled it. She turned to me, her eyes filling half her face.

"May I please have raita?" she breathed in a voice tradition-ally used for negotiating items from the Frito-Lay group. I noted the sign that read "Raita: $6.00 a pint." That seemed more like a fresh-raspberry price, not a food-typically-eaten-by-grad-students-because-it-is-filling-and-cheap price. So I questioned the owner, who gave me a spirited lecture about the cost of cre-ating healthy, locally raised food while also paying workers a living wage. Cowed, I asked if there was a smaller size. But, no, apparently one can only appreciate yogurt with fair-trade things floating in it in pint-sized containers.

I said to Alice, "If I get it . . . ," and she fist-pumped "Yes!" She assumed this was the "If" that meant *I'm finding a way to give you what you want while still maintaining the illusion that I run the place*. But when I spend six dollars on gelatinous yogurt, it will come with conditions, so I continued, "If I get it, you have to eat it. All of it." On the off chance I wasn't flogging the subject sufficiently, I added, "I don't eat raita, so if I buy it, you are telling me you will eat it. It's expensive."

"I will. I will. Thank you," she chanted, eyes fixed on the ice chest holding the nectar. I handed over six dollars and got my pint of Indian white. The owner warned me that the food was freshly made without preservatives and as such needed to be eaten within two days, which certainly didn't seem to be a problem, since Alice kept opening the bag and affectionately patting the container of raita as if it were a guinea pig.

She ate the entire pint of lentils that night for dinner, which gave me the narcotic rush of *Look at me, raising a child who en-joys healthy, vegetarian food. I don't know why people think this*

mothering business is so hard. Really, just a little care and atten-
tion, and children dance to your bidding.

I had now set up all the pins. Karma picked up her bowling ball.

The next night we ate dinner out. The following evening, as I pulled the raita from the fridge, its expiration date looming in my thoughts, I asked Alice, "Do you want your raita over lentils and rice?"

"Yeah," she replied. "I guess." This wasn't the same girl who had been liquid yogurt's head cheerleader less than forty-eight hours earlier. No worries, I told myself. She'll come around once she gazes upon its pearlescent splendor. I heated the lentils and rice and poured some of the cool raita on the side of the plate, which I placed in front of my daughter. She set upon the rice and lentils like some kind of botanic predator. I waited; the raita remained untouched. In fact, if I had to give a sworn deposition, I would have said the raita was being avoided.

"Didn't you notice? Raita. On your plate," I said stupidly, as if the goop leaching into her rice was visible only to me. She moved a raita-dribbled grain of rice onto her fork and between her lips. She looked at me, her lip curled slightly. I barked, "What?" To which she said, "I'd like it if weren't for the vegetables in it."

I exhaled slowly through my teeth and said in my dangerously even tone, "It had the same vegetables in it when you couldn't live without it two days ago. Just. Eat. It."

She ate another grain of rice, which, possibly, had abutted a grain of rice that had touched the raita, and then she looked at me. "I'm full," she announced. "You can have the rest."

"I don't want the rest. I never wanted the rest. I want you to eat it. I paid good money for that raita . . ."

"*Good money*." There's a phrase. Of course I'd heard it before having a child—had heard it *as* a child—but I don't believe I'd actually used it until I had a child. Roughly translated, "good money" means: "Money can be spent only once. If I spend it on a music class but you spend said class braiding and re-braiding your hair I start fixating on how the same money could have purchased one of those salon afternoons where they massage my neck before they wash my hair and then offer me a glass of wine while it's being cut, so allow me the delusion that you are actually gaining something from the money I spend on you . . ."

"And if you think you are going to be allowed to waste food . . ."

"Waste," like "good money," is a loaded term in my house. A woman with leftover containers dedicated to archiving two tablespoons of uneaten dinner isn't inclined to view an uneaten pint of six-dollar yogurt as a good thing.

"You are sorely mistaken." I could have ended there, but I continued, "I expect you to take responsibility for your choices . . ."

And there it was. When you grow up in a city that venerates eternal adolescence, you are more likely to see a snow leopard than someone who takes responsibility for her own actions. Even if, by the grace of God or irrefutable videotaped evidence, someone admits that yes, they *did* whatever thing they are being accused of, there's always the "But . . ."

. . . I had been taking medication for a neck injury.

. . . You didn't hear what he said to me first.

. . . I only requested a therapeutic massage.

Alice might live in Los Angeles, and she might get to know firsthand its endless beaches and American Girl emporium, but my daughter doesn't get to "Yes, but" her way out of personal responsibility. Today, expensive raita. Ten years from now, her PR people are explaining how that Ecuadorian family of six leapt in front of her car. I was about to find some way of explaining this to her when I caught her expression. The forkful of raita and rice was next to her trembling lips, under her huge liquid eyes; if an artist ever wanted to create the definitive portrayal of what misery looks like on a child's face, I had the model.

I stood there, frozen. We had reached an impasse, and I had no idea what to do. Clearly she wasn't going to eat the whole pint, now or ever. If I forced her to eat it, she'd probably develop a complex about dairy products, or grow up to hate everything Indian. I could ruin her relationship with an entire subcontinent. On the other hand, if I gave up and let her leave the table, the lesson she would learn is "appear tragic enough and Mommy folds." The next thing you know, she's standing in Saks Fifth Avenue holding up a thousand-dollar handbag and whimpering, "But Mommy, all the other Girl Scouts have it, and you wouldn't want me to feel *sad*, would you?"

For the sake of any future negotiations, she had to eat some. But how much? Did one bite achieve the holy trinity of not wasting my money, not wasting food, and not wasting a chance to become a moral person? That's a lot to put on one bite. Maybe she needed to take two. But just then, a little cloud started to form over my heart. Did the fact that I was caving in from "You must eat it all, every single bite, I mean it and I'm not backing down" to "Okay, two bites, two is fine," make me no better than a mother at the grocery store offering to buy Ho Hos if her son stops kicking her?

This, in case you're curious, is why most parenting magazines write articles about the problems of infants and toddlers. Teaching them not to bite can be covered in a 750-word article, because nearly all the behavior of that age, no matter how unsightly, resolves itself and is soon replaced by even less sanitary habits. The quandaries of raising older children can't even be fully described in 750 words, much less resolved. These are the moments of my life when I not only feel like a well-meaning but bumbling idiot—my default setting—but I actually feel utterly alone. (Do I even need to say that her father was out for the evening?)

I was left with the same question, the one that flattens me every time: *What is enough?* There comes a point in every disciplinary action where things can slip too easily from "These are the consequences of your actions" to "Years from now, your therapy group is going to love this." Obviously, I am not talking about physical or emotional abuse; I'm talking about two people in a room and maybe one of them has always wondered what makes the clacking sound when you shake nail polish and decides to answer that question once and for all by pouring the nail polish on the bedspread, and now the other one has to decide exactly how much punishment she needs to inflict. (That wasn't Alice, by the way. That was me. I was six. The noise comes from ball bearings.)

I read all the parenting books, some twice. I know the best parent is a consistent, loving, authoritative presence. You tell each child, every day, in large ways and small, "These are the things that matter to me and will eventually matter to you.

Please behave in this fashion." And you understand that as the parent you have to keep advocating for the expected behavior all the time. We always say "please" and "thank you." We always make our bed in the morning. We never use Mommy's toothbrush to get the cat looking her best. But children, wily and alert little devils that they are, spend many years looking for loopholes, and life keeps conspiring to create them. Over the years, they learn that certain rules are only in effect around their grandmothers but can be ignored at other times. They learn that after Daddy has driven for an hour on the freeway and only gone two-tenths of a mile, he doesn't care what you do, as long as you do it quietly. They learn that for one week a month Mommy has a much more stringent definition of the phrase "back talk" and a much lower tolerance for it. What I want to be is a strong, resolute figure leading my daughter through the primeval forest of childhood, hacking out a clear, bright path of expectations for her. What I usually end up being is a person swatting at bugs, squinting at the sun and saying nervously, "Wait. I know I have the map here somewhere."

In the end, Alice choked down three bites, one for each character trait I was trying to impress upon her. Also, she had to pay me for the raita she urged me to buy but now didn't want. Her loathing of the stuff was so profound she didn't even look miffed at the loss of hard-earned capital. We lived through another mothering moment with only the odd psychic abrasion and some cucumber floating in a cup of soured milk as a reminder.

The dog wouldn't eat it either.

Like Nature Intended

I CANNOT SAY THAT BEING A CHILD ACTOR WAS DETRIMEN-
tal to me, but I could have done without being a *former* child
actor. To be a child is a temporary condition. To be a former child
actor is a permanent state. Former child actors aren't people.
They're memories from your childhood, little people who lived
in the television in the den. It would be as if I asked you to consider the feelings of an EASY-BAKE Oven.

Former child actors are frequently exposed to idiotic questions. They are required to respond graciously when people ask
them things they wouldn't have the nerve to ask their brother-
in-law after drinking a six-pack. Do you have any money left or
did your parents spend it all? Was (actor with whom I worked)
an ass? and Did acting ruin your life?

I try to be polite. I tell people that my parents spent every
cent I made on cheap wine and aboveground swimming pools,
and what a comfort it is to discuss this with them, a complete
stranger. I tell them that (Actor with whom I worked) was a
lovely person, but he was an adult and I was a child so, outside
of acting, our interests didn't exactly coincide. I couldn't legally
meet him at a nightclub and he wasn't too excited about hanging out with me while I read the Little House on the Prairie
books, ate Wheat Thins, and drank Tom Collins mixer. As to
the *did-acting-ruin-your-life* question—the answer is no. Actually, I liked acting and acting suited my personality quite well,

which says nothing good about my character. I remember once getting very upset with my mother for using something funny I had said without giving me credit. I barged into the adults' conversation and said through gritted teeth, "That was my line, you know." I was six years old; I wasn't even acting yet.

The maddening part about being a former child actor is that I'm not *always* a former child actor. If I look good and I'm not perspiring copiously or in the middle of saying something inappropriate, no one recognizes me. I'm just another civilian with a fresh manicure. As luck would have it, I'm rarely composed and I'm usually disheveled. If Rupert the dog has made a break for it and I'm running down the street in my pajamas screaming, "Come BACK here you (verb form of expletive) (noun expletive) hellhound or I swear to (verb form of expletive) (deity) I'm going to beat you into a PASTE!" and I stop to gasp and sweat and pull bees out of my feet, someone getting out of a car will look at me, smile, and say, "I'm sorry, but weren't you—?" I blot my brow and try to be gracious because that person hasn't done anything wrong in wanting to confirm that I was, and still am, Quinn Cummings, and it doesn't hurt me to be polite—most of the time.

At the height of the dot-com frenzy, I took a job in San Francisco. After several weeks of dead ends, I left Los Angeles without having a place to live in San Francisco. I figured I'd get there, stay in a hotel for a few days, find a sublet, and move in. That seemed like the kind of whimsical thing people I knew did all the time, and it always worked out fabulously for them. I had forgotten that whimsy, like paisley, is incredibly unflattering on me. There was, quite literally, no housing to be had in the entire city.

I gave up quickly on finding a whole apartment, then on finding a room in a house, then a spare bedroom in an apartment.

I was down to begging strangers to let me drop an air mattress in a hallway and contemplating the more picturesque Dumpsters near South Park when a Los Angeles friend called with an offer. His cousin and her girlfriend were going to Europe and needed someone to watch their apartment and take care of their cat for two weeks. I went to meet the women. The apartment was a cozy, rundown sort of place, covered in cat hair and located directly behind San Francisco General Hospital, thus assuring me a constant wail of sirens. Then again, it wasn't the backseat of my car, and it bought me two more weeks to try to find a proper sublet. My responsibilities as temporary tenant were simple: bring in the mail; answer the phone as needed; give the cat her IV drip.

I'm sorry, what?

The women had tried for several years to have a child. When it became apparent this wasn't going to happen, the cat became their beloved offspring. Unfortunately, the cat was now very old; every major organ system was fading like a Hawaiian sunset. Her eyes were cloudy, her hearing was shot, and her kidneys were failing by the minute so unless she was rehydrated and fed twenty dollars' worth of medication twice every day, she would die.

You know, like nature intended.

I received a swooningly vivid demonstration of how to pick up the cat (which, while really sweet, resembled something you'd collect on a Swiffer), pinch up the skin on her neck, and plunge in the needle. She let out a weak but truculent mew. I let out a half-choked whimper. Next, I was taught how to pulverize her heart pill, mix it with water, put it into a syringe, and jam it down her throat.

For the next two weeks, I awoke at five every morning and, before I went to the gym, stumbled around the apartment trying to find Linty the cat. Sometimes, I would grab under the bed only to snatch up a dust bunny or a limp sock. Eventually I would locate her slumped form somewhere in the apartment, and she would emit this little moan, which said plainly, "Crap. Still alive."

Every morning and every night, I would insert the IV line and wait for the bag of fluid to empty into her. Every morning and every night I would watch her minimal life force come back as the fluid rehydrated her. Every morning and every night I would remember that she hated her heart pills and that I should have given them to her first, when she was still walking toward the light. Every morning, I would leave for the gym with paper towels worn around my arms like blood-specked dropcloths, absorbing the vivid reminders of exactly how much she hated heart pills.

It is a testimony to the housing situation in San Francisco that I still considered myself lucky.

During this time, I had found a longer-term temporary housing situation (the housemate of a high-school friend's ex-girlfriend had been popped for shoplifting for the third time. He jumped bail. His room was free. Whee!) so when Linty's moms returned, I moved out that afternoon. As I was packing, one of the women invited me back the following night for her birthday party. I didn't really know anyone in town besides the stock-optioned teenagers I was working with, and I was still thankful they had taken me in, so I gladly accepted.

When I arrived the next evening, the apartment was full of women. I smiled politely, slid through to the kitchen, got myself a drink. As I was coming back into the living room, the girl-friend of the birthday girl grabbed me by the wrist and tugged me toward the birthday girl, who was standing by the fireplace. Assuming she wanted me to wish her girlfriend a happy birth-day, I went along without hesitation. Why wouldn't I? They were middle-aged lesbians in San Francisco. The worst thing that should have happened to me was being forced to try lentil and hummus pâté.

Once I was standing between the hostesses, the birthday girl called out, "Excuse me? Everyone? Be quiet!"

The rest of the women in the room quieted down and stared expectantly at their beaming hostesses, and at me sandwiched between them. My stomach sank.

"I'm sure you all remember *The Goodbye Girl* . . ."

No, I'm thinking frantically, she's not going to do this.

"The little know-it-all on *Family*, you remember that show?"

The women started conferring. Some remembered it, some needed their memories refreshed, some had no idea what she was talking about. All of them, however, were staring at us with great interest. My expression was probably similar to the time I stuck my foot in my rollerblade and discovered half of a fat liz-ard my cat had secreted in there for some later meal.

"Anyway, here's our friend, the little child star, Quinn Cum-mings!"

She hugged me, and then stepped back a bit so that her friends could fully appreciate my former child star aura. My first thought was: If this is what they did to their friends, what did they do to mere acquaintances? Ritualized flaying?

One woman brayed, "So, who did you work with who was lesbian? Is (the name of an actress) a dyke?"

The women chorused, "Yes! Who's gay?"

I was near paralysis in horror and anger at this behavior. Still, I managed to come up with a nearly Victorian "I'm *sure* I wouldn't know who is gay or lesbian. It wouldn't *occur* to me to ask." [Lies, lies, lies. I know all *sorts* of things about all *sorts* of people. Some are out. Some are not. Some live discreet lives as homosexuals or bisexuals. Some are off-the-charts sluts. But if you think I was going to out someone for the satisfaction of these nattering harpies, you are painfully mistaken.]

Once everyone figured out that the former child star wasn't going to do some adorable tricks, the interest in me faded a bit. I took this opportunity to slither out of the room and make a break for the front door. Sure, it was rude not to say good-bye to the hosts, but *they started it*.

I got to my new apartment and went back to unpacking when a horrible thought occurred to me. I checked the bags. I checked my car. I checked my bags again. Oh, hell, I had left my good winter coat at the Cat House. I had to go back for the coat, but if I saw those two women again, I was going to say something awful, something I might regret. Actually, I wouldn't regret it at all, and I'd probably play what I said back again and again in my head and giggle, but I wanted to believe I was a better person than that. I tried to tap into my inner San Franciscan, a mellow forgiving individual who could listen to the Grateful Dead without wanting to slam her hand in a door.

An hour later I was back at their house. They only lived ten minutes away from my new place; the other fifty minutes had been spent trying to find a parking space, which did absolutely nothing to foster a "live and forgive" attitude in my heart. I ran up to the apartment, now empty except for the hostesses and, I assume, Linty the cat. I found my coat, brushed off the larger pyramids of cat fur, and inhaled deeply to begin my prepared speech. I then coughed out a Hindenburg of hair, and tried again.

"Look, I don't want to make a big deal about this, but you two did something that made me . . ."

I thought about the words I wanted to use: "blindingly irritated"? "teeth-gnashingly irked"?

I went with: "kind of uncomfortable."

They stared blankly at me so I continued. "It was very nice of you to invite me to your party, but when you brought me up in the front of the room like that, and introduced me as a former child star, I felt like the evening's entertainment."

I waited for some expression of embarrassment to cross their faces. They waited patiently, expecting me to come to the point where they had committed a faux pas. I tried again.

"That part of my life was nearly two decades ago, and when it's the first thing someone finds worth mentioning about me, I start to feel as if I have done nothing else of any consequence in my life."

An exquisite pause occurred, where we all wondered if anyone was going to leap in and protest that I had done lots of worthwhile things after puberty. No one did.

The birthday girl protested, "But everyone wanted to hear about Hollywood."

Her girlfriend lay a protective hand on her shoulder.

"Honey, let Quinn vent."

LET.
QUINN.
VENT?

Venting is something you do when traffic is really bad and you come home and yell at your spouse for fifteen minutes about how you want to live in a city with two thousand people and where you can walk to work.

Venting is something you do at a bar after everyone has watched the presidential debates.

Venting is when the person doing the venting is being slightly irrational and the person being vented at is blameless.

Two hours before, these people wanted me to tap out my age with my hoof for a roomful of strangers, and I was *venting*?

Neither of these women, who between them had five master's degrees, thought the situation merited an "I'm sorry." I didn't even get an "I'm sorry you feel that way," which wouldn't technically qualify as an apology anyway.

I gripped my coat and said icily, "Guess my *venting* is done." I spun on my heel and headed for the door. In my path was the dispirited balding lump of fur that was my former patient. I leaned over and scratched her head. She purred. I yanked the door open and headed down the street toward my car, marinating in the pleasure of being of no interest to anyone at all.

The Next Dolph Lundgren

WHEN I WAS IN MY EARLY TWENTIES AND LIFE'S WIDE PO-
tential still flirted with me and took my calls, I tried other jobs
in the entertainment industry. For me, acting had totally passed
its sell-by date. I didn't like it anymore and if the total lack of job
offers was any clue, acting wasn't so fond of me either. But damn
it, I liked being around creative types. They were emotionally
damaged, immature, fearful, grandiose, and prone to dressing
far too young for their age but as far as I was concerned they
were family and I wasn't prepared to give up on them yet.

My first thought was, *I'll become a sitcom writer because they
ingest sugar and caffeine by the barrel and I'm good at that already.* As far as I knew, sitcom writers sat in a windowless office
for days on end, being fed a constant drip of Red Vines and Thai
food to keep their blood pumping while they debated which
word was inherently funnier: "kneecap" or "Schenectady." If the
writers worked on a cable sitcom, the debated words would be
obscene and the Red Vines would be the cheap generic kind,
which tasted nearly the same. Cable writers still got Thai food.
Either way, this was a good life to my way of thinking. I'd be
gainfully employed in show business and my grocery bills would
be nonexistent. I commenced to writing.

This plan had several flaws. For one thing, the entertainment industry needs far fewer writers than actors. For another,
writing a spec sitcom while huddled in the dark, spider-saturated

back room of a house you are sharing with what seemed like 115 people didn't ease the I'm-becoming-a-weird-little-shut-in-about-a-minute-away-from-writing-a-manifesto-and-wearing-mayonnaise-as-foundation concerns I'd been struggling with for several months. I'd sit in that darkened cobwebby room for hours on end, frowning at a computer screen, eating pretzels, and preparing for the magical day when I'd be handsomely paid for frowning at a computer screen and eating pretzels. At the sound of any human voice in the vicinity, I would drop all creative efforts, emerge from my cave squinting at the daylight, brush the spiders from my eyelashes, and talk about anything to anyone I found lounging by the pool. The loungers were more than glad to keep the conversational ball aloft as long as I was willing to talk about being high, house music, or the joys of listening to house music while being high.

On paper, I had one housemate. In reality, I had one housemate, his boyfriend, a handful of their college friends eager to see how many brain cells they could destroy before starting grad school, and a claque of random characters my housemate had met at a bar the previous evening. The common denominators were that they were all attractive, they all lived off trust funds, and they all had the work ethic of runny cheese. Most had vague aspirations toward creating art as long as creating art didn't conflict with being attractive, getting high, hanging out in bars, and having carnal knowledge of complete strangers. Discouragingly enough for those of us who want to believe that good work habits matter in life, many of these people went on to earn vast sums of money while still finding the time to continue to be attractive, get really high, hang out in bars, and have carnal knowledge of complete strangers.

I walked outside to mingle with that day's sybarites. Someone was using skills he received completing his MFA to sculpt a bong from a cantaloupe. It was passed around. Inhalation occurred. Minutes later, someone said dreamily, "We should get a . . . pizza."

Silence. The guy who made the suggestion looked worried. "Did I just say that out loud?"

Heads nodded dreamily.

"It is called a *pizza*, right?"

Everyone besides me pondered. Eventually, someone nodded. Yes, that's what it's called. The CD player, showing more industry than anyone around the pool, slipped from one George Michael tune to the next. I fidgeted in my lounge chair.

I had spent the first part of the day with a handful of attractive and quick-witted twenty-somethings who, while they existed only in my head, knew when they were talking out loud, knew their problems could be resolved in twenty-two minutes, and knew the word for pizza. These three-dimensional characters didn't strike me as believable. Having had enough of the real world, I ran back to the sanctuary of my computer and my spiders. I had grown fond of those spiders. I had even named some of them. A few more months of this and I'd be taking their suggestions for dialogue. Perhaps I needed to reconsider my pre-midlife-crisis career change.

Looking back, I think I was ambivalent about starting at the bottom, down in the sitcom bogs. This is not because I thought I was too grand for an entry-level assignment. No, my great fear was that my writing was just good enough to get me in at the bottom, and I would stay there forever, eventually becoming its queen. This fear was not completely irrational. Once, during a meeting, a television executive who had read my sample scripts leaned across her desk and said to me, "You're good."

I tried to find an expression that said, while modest about it, I heard this all the time, and not just from my office spiders.

She continued, "You're not just good. You're *Saved by the Bell* good."

I waited for the laugh to follow. She was joking, dear God let her be joking. Her expression of having bestowed upon me a great blessing didn't change. For months afterward, I was haunted by the specter that if I worked hard and had a massive stroke of good luck I might—just possibly—write a sitcom episode that worked in a special appearance by Carrot Top.

In the end, I didn't stay with sitcom writing because that career path wasn't helpful. I wanted to help. I wanted to be of service. Thanks to ninety-hour workweeks, sitcom writers are only of service when lavishly tipping the Thai-food guy. I couldn't wait that long. I had to help now. Hiding the pets so my housemates wouldn't get them stoned was a benevolent act but not quite enough. The answer came to me as I frowned, talked to spiders, and struggled for punch lines: I'd become a talent agent. Yes, that's it. I'd represent actors, using my lifetime of experience in the entertainment industry to protect and serve these talented, fragile artists. The sheer simple genius of my idea caused me to stop, midword. God, it was so perfect, so logical, so helpful.

And so wrong. I spent about two years and nearly all my remaining goodwill being a talent agent. The agency where I worked was not big but it was prestigious. We had a small roster of clients who continue to win awards and critical acclaim on a regular basis. We had a larger roster of clients whose faces make you stop and think, "Wasn't he in my sister-in-law's wedding party?" The actors I represented were worthy people and, for the most part, genuinely talented. They deserved a good agent. Sadly, they got me. Having a twisted need to be of service wasn't enough to make me good at my job or even competent. For one thing, I have an almost phobic distaste for discussing money. If you are the person negotiating contracts, you shouldn't get sweaty at the thought of talking about money. You shouldn't have to give yourself weird little pep talks just to get up the nerve to say "Mr. Casting Director, I'm sorry to interrupt your speech on what an important and meaningful script this is, and I hate to not be all about the art, but the actors are actually going to get paid, right?"

Frequently, the answer to this was "Um . . ."

Our agency divided the work not by the actor but by the medium so, in theory, I handled every client up to and including the Academy Award winners for my corner of the industry. Of course, by the time I became an agent all the good corners were covered. Two agents covered studio projects and two agents covered television. What's left? I'll tell you what's left: indies.

When I was hired, I imagined a life of impassioned advocacy; of bringing exactly the right actor to the attention of a young and brilliant independent filmmaker who would give us all a reason to go to Sundance next year. In reality, my projects fell into three categories: God-awful but financed; Wonderful but never-going-to-get-financed; and Horrible and being-shot-next-week-in-Bulgaria. Always, mystifyingly, Bulgaria. At least once a month I would be handed a script about half-naked teen-agers being terrorized by a giant red ant in a small Midwestern town (which was going to end up looking suspiciously like Sofia, Bulgaria). This movie inevitably starred someone like Morgan Fairchild, on whom the producers had spent their lavish casting budget.

That was the other pleasure of my movies: if I was very lucky, they actually paid Screen Actors Guild minimum wage. Most of the time, the original casting sheet would say "Salary deferred," which meant we all were supposed to buy into the collective hallucination that a 16-mm art film about a struggling writer/director in Los Angeles (played by the writer/director) and his devoted, incredibly hot, frequently naked girlfriend (to be hired after multiple auditions) was going to dazzle the festival circuit, be picked up for distribution by Miramax, and then, hoo boy, wouldn't the money roll in!

Such was my life. Most clients passed on the scripts I covered, and I couldn't say I blamed them.

And then there was Dick. His name isn't really Dick but I'm going to call him that because I was Ahab and he was my great white whale. He was a terrifically gifted actor who seemed to take some profound pleasure in not acting. The man passed on every single project I had going, even the ones that didn't make me want to leave the script at the bottom of a lye pit. I didn't take it too personally because he passed on nearly every television interview my colleagues set up, as well as a few high-budget studio pictures. He felt strongly about acting only in projects he found compelling and he'd created a life where he could do just that. Other clients, after being out of work a few months, would start calling, first casually and then more frantically, re-

minding their agents of their mortgages, their children's school-
ing, their ex-wives, and their gambling debts. They, too, had
high artistic standards but they also had the moral flexibility to
take a guest-starring credit on *Full House*.

Not Dick. He had broad shoulders, a full head of hair, no
costly bad habits, and no dependents. Casting directors would
call asking for him. I would leave him a message to pick up a
copy of the script. Days later, he would drift by and collect it.
Weeks later, after avoiding calls, he would leave a 2:00 a.m.
voice mail passing on the audition. He would then compound
my aggravation by leaving a message with the receptionist explaining that he would be unavailable for three weeks because he
was off to star in—and also haul props for—a friend's independent movie to be shot in the Sonoran Desert where there was no
cell-phone coverage.

The whale would evade me again.

Finally, *finally*, I got a script worth something. True, it was
an independent film with no studio attached to release it, but
there were actual, reputable actors signed, as opposed to many
of my projects that starred Dolph Lundgren or, more depress-
ingly, someone described as "the next Dolph Lundgren." This
was the real deal. The script was funny, the director wasn't the
son-in-law of the financier, and, the most thrilling news of all:
they were paying more than union scale.

I developed a nosebleed from excitement.

Best of all, there was a perfect role for Dick, an actor capable
of flawless comedic timing while shirtless. I submitted his picture and received no response, which isn't surprising, considering how in three days the casting director probably received five
hundred headshots for that one part alone, and there were forty

roles to fill. I started working the phone. I pleaded, flirted, begged, nagged, and cajoled. Not the casting director, mind you; she knew better than to answer her own phone. I may have propositioned the cleaning crew. But something in my cringing and whining tone must have worked because I got Dick in for an interview. I threw myself into the boat and headed out to the high seas to find my white whale.

I managed to locate him, convince him to call me back, pick up the script, and read it within a week. This set some sort of land-speed record. The good luck continued; he agreed to audition. I had the whale in my sight! He read for the part and the director fell in love with him. The casting director called me within an hour to offer the role, with a salary that would actually buy more than ramen noodles and Tang.

My hands shook when I called him. Barely able to conceal my glee, I told him he booked the job, that the money was not bad, and that he would be shooting in two weeks.

"Yeah," he said absentmindedly, "I forgot to tell you. I promised my friend Ace that I would help him with his movie. I'm going to be in Riverside, on and off, for the rest of the month."

Wave good-bye to the nice whale, Ahab.

No, he wouldn't consider bailing out on his friend; that wouldn't be right. Besides, it was a really cool script about speed-dealing bikers who spoke in blank verse. Half the characters would be sock puppets.

I got the phone number of the producer of Ace's movie, a person I suspect was also Ace's mother. She gave me Dick's shooting schedule—contingent, of course, on the sock puppets being mended in time. I then called the production manager of what I had come to think of as the *real* movie and got every single day Dick would be needed on set. They overlapped by two days. I went back and forth between the two people, trying desperately to get one to adjust his or her schedule.

It took the better part of a day, but I finally had the sock puppet producer offering to shoot Dick from 12:00 to 3:00 a.m., and the real movie's production manager saying he wouldn't schedule Dick to the set any earlier than six hours later. It was horrible, but my client was young enough to handle a long day in the name of art and a union gig.

Laughing in relief, I called Dick and, swelling with well-earned pride, I walked him through the schedule. I don't know what I was expecting, but it certainly wasn't him drawling, "Yeah, but if Ace needs me to help, I'm going to have to stay."

Help? Help what? Put the other actors back in the sock drawer? I put down the phone and slammed into another agent's office for advice.

This agent, call her Medusa, had been doing this forever. If you caught her on a good day she was personable and well-seasoned. The other 363 days of the year she was a wolverine with a toothache. The pot she smoked to take the edge off didn't seem to help. If anything, it made her forgetful and paranoid. The one thing she never forgot, sadly, was that she couldn't stand me. All I had to do was walk into a room where she was and she'd let out an involuntary "Oh, God." So, of course, I felt compelled to somehow make myself less repellent in her eyes, which meant I spent more time insinuating myself near her, which just annoyed her more. After nearly a year, I had finally come to the conclusion that I could continue to question why I got under her skin, but it would be just as productive as wondering if a Komodo dragon was going for my eyes because it had unresolved family issues. Both the lizard and Medusa were best given plenty of room. Still, she had years of experience on me, and I had run out of ideas. My modest hope, as always when I had to talk to Medusa, was "the bare minimum of screaming, please." On most occasions, the way it went was I'd talk, she'd scream at me, I'd wilt from the fog of her hostility and slink away.

That was another reason I was a dreadful agent. Any agent worth their Armani suit must be aggressive. Extremely aggressive. All the time. They fight for parts for their clients, they fight to attract new clients and keep old ones, they fight for money. The family crest of the best Hollywood agent would show a fat wallet, an airplane ticket to Park City, and a set of bared teeth. I hate conflict so much I will drive two blocks out of my way to avoid passing a restaurant where I had an uncomfortable conversation. Had I taken that high school test that indicates which career path one should follow, it would have come back as "Hermit."

Medusa was talking to her dealer on the phone and motioned for me to leave. I waited and bounced from foot to foot. When I made it clear I wasn't going, she hung up and glowered at me.

"What?"

After that warm welcome, I explained my problem. I produced a piece of paper to show the simple brilliance of the schedule I had gotten two strangers to agree upon. I then finished up with my client's maddening reply. Medusa looked at me with a weary distaste, which was the best possible reaction I excited in her.

"Quinn, you can't want it more than they do."

I froze. Her brain might have had the same chemical makeup as the air over a Phish concert, but this was the most insightful thing I had ever heard anyone say. As if entranced, I walked back to my office, called the producer of the real movie, and told him Dick had dates locked in place from a previous commitment. These were either to be worked around or we would have to pass on the part. Somehow, they managed. Dick shot both movies.

The sock-puppet movie was never seen again. Unfortunately, neither was the real movie. A decade later, I occasionally see Dick in a film doing a wonderful job. I silently toast whatever Ahab caught him.

The only things I've taken away from that period of my life are a pair of seemingly unkillable gray flannel trousers, a lifelong distaste for Bulgaria, and the lesson Medusa taught me that afternoon. I look at everyone dear to me and I am desperate to fix them. Desperate. Someone starts complaining about how their clothes don't fit, or how their doctor is after them to bring down their cholesterol, or about how useless their boyfriend is, and I leap into the fray. Here's a diet! Here's a map of all the hikes in Los Angeles! Here's a way to start the conversation with the useless boyfriend that will lead to him moving out! I'm lousy at fixing my own problems, but other people's problems? Let me at 'em.

Until the other person says, "Yeah . . ." in the die-away voice, which means, "I like talking about this, but I don't dislike this situation enough to actually do something about it."

Sometimes I will forget Medusa's lesson. I'll try to nag and pester the person into a state of improvement that just seems to

annoy everyone involved. And then, out of the blue, I will hear her smoke-throttled voice saying, "You can't want it more than they do," and I will stop midharangue and say something along the lines of, "If you ever want help, let me know."

I've modified Medusa's credo a bit over the years. If the outcome is something that affects you and the other person, you can want it as much as they do. You can even want it more, but only briefly. If two people are in something together, they each have to pull their own weight. But if it isn't *your* goal, don't take on the responsibility for achieving it. You can only help someone as much as they genuinely want to be helped.

I think that's what the spiders were trying to tell me.

Something Inappropriate About Canada

WHEN CONSORT AND I FIRST STARTED DATING AND WERE shin deep in the *Oh, aren't you just the most wonderful thing! How amusingly you breathe!* flush of romance, we attended a fancy party. Later, on the way home, he turned to me and said, "You know what's so great about you?" I shrugged, hoping it wasn't something like *The way you hide those fat ankles.*

"How equally comfortable you are with everybody," he continued. "Every time I looked over, there you were chatting away with some new person." This was indeed a compliment. To Consort, thumbs and graceful small talk are what separate us from the animals. I modestly accepted this tribute to my outgoing nature as we drove through the shiny urban nightscape.

About a year later, when Consort still loved me but the warm bath of bond-inducing chemicals had worn off, that previous conversation came up. He squinted affectionately and said, "I was wrong. It's not that you're equally comfortable with nearly everyone. It's that you're equally *uncomfortable* with nearly everyone."

Well, yes. There's that.

What separates me from other shy people is that I am an actor by training; I'm practiced in the arts of public deception and entertaining sound bites. In fact, a significant part of my energy is spent *not* appearing as uncomfortable as I feel. For me, appearing at ease and relaxed is exhausting. This is because no matter how well everything is going, I know that I am seconds away from saying something horrible.

I have never gotten high on pot. I don't say this out of a desire to run for Congress (although I would appreciate your vote), or because I think marijuana is the demon leaf. Statistics prove that alcohol is a far more dangerous drug, and I'm doing my best to keep that industry vibrant. No, the reason I don't smoke pot is because all through my adolescence I kept hearing stories about the effects of getting high; specifically, about getting stoned and fixating over whether you were not talking enough, or talking too much, or saying out loud what was meant to stay in your head, or whether you were making any sense at all. All I could think was: *other people need drugs for that?*

Somewhere within my brain resides an eighteen-month-old child. I know this because when Alice was right around that age she became obsessed with mauling our then-dog Polly's tail. Polly had come to us when Alice was six months old and Polly was about seven years old—the shelter wasn't exactly sure. Polly had been owned by an elderly woman with whom she watched daytime television and ate snacks. This explained her build. When Alice first set eyes on her, she shrieked in delight. Alice, that is. Polly assumed a look of polite horror, which told us our new family pet hadn't spent much time around actual children. Fortunately, for a dog with minimal small-child experience, Polly took quite gracefully to being loved well but not wisely by the under-three crowd. She was generally patient and accommodating with Alice and her elfin friends, except for one thing: no one—repeat, *no one*—was to touch her tail.

As far as Polly was concerned, her tail was like the parts of one's body covered by a bathing suit. She, and she alone, got to decide who touched it, and to our best knowledge she never met anyone who merited such favor. Of course, this made her tail unbearably desirable to my newly running daughter. She wanted to touch it, pull it, sing to it, and use it as dental floss. At least twenty-five times a day, twenty of which were while I was trying to make dinner, Alice would make a running lunge for Polly's tail. Polly, sensing disaster, would tuck her tail where only she could find it and race for her bed. My daughter, the thrill of the hunt exciting her blood, would shriek and chase her prey while I called after her, "Alice, don't touch Polly's tail. Leave her tail alone."

What my Alice would hear was "Alice . . . (inaudible sound) . . . touch Polly's tail . . . (inaudible) (inaudible) . . . TAIL . . . (inaudible)."

Everything else on the dog, being available to Alice, was dreary. That tail, by sheer virtue of its being forbidden, was better than ten My Little Ponies, an afternoon at the park, and themed footwear all wrapped up with a big purple bow made of candy. That's how my brain works too. The mere suggestion of "don't," especially when it precedes any sort of social prohibition such as "Don't say something stupid," "Don't say something weird," or "Don't say something stupid *or* weird," and my brain takes on the gravitational characteristics of Jupiter. This is a state whereby a random thought, especially a random thought with ample fuel for embarrassment, gets sucked in from the black abyss of space and shoots right out of my mouth. In the natural laws that shape my world, this force is especially strong when strangers are present. Upon meeting someone for the first time, I might notice something about them that is completely out of the range of polite conversation and, of course, this becomes all I can think to talk about.

Quinn meets new person. This woman has a luxurious
moustache.

NEW PERSON: Hello, Quinn. It's nice to meet you.

QUINN'S BRAIN: MOUSTACHE!

QUINN'S MOUTH: So nice to meet you.

Have you been to the Frida Kahlo show?

NEW PERSON: Uh, no. Why?

QUINN: I . . . thought maybe I had seen you there.

It's . . . good . . .

Agonizing silence.

QUINN'S BRAIN: MOUSTACHE!

QUINN'S MOUTH: You should try to see it.

NEW PERSON: I will.

More agonizing silence. We both sip our drinks.
She looks for other people who might save her from me.
I look anywhere but at her upper lip, where I swear
her moustache is leering at me.

New person gives up waiting and bolts for freedom,
her moustache waving in the breeze.

At the start of Alice's preschool career, I made an offhand
remark to her teacher, something to the effect that I thought another child was behaving like Satan. (Oh, stop looking at me
like that. If you knew this kid you'd have said it too.) Turns out,
this sweet woman, being a devout Christian and all, took some

offense with my having referred to an innocent (ha!) child as the Dark Lord of Hell. So I apologized, sincerely. And, to the degree that I regretted having made the teacher uncomfortable, I meant it. (I do, however, stand by my assertion. Trust me, this kid reeked of sulfur.) So, could someone please explain to me why, for the next two years, I could not speak to this teacher without injecting sin or perdition into every conversation? There was no subject so ordinary that I couldn't drag malediction into it somehow. "Sorry, I'm late, but the traffic was hellish. It was evil and Godless. And damned if I could get a single green light."

To which the nice Christian teacher could only reply, "I'll be praying for you."

It's not just the Christians or the hirsute. If I meet observant Muslims, I'll blurt out something about the joys of bacon. If I meet someone in a wheelchair, I'll drone on about how much I'm enjoying the treadmill these days. If the other person is blind, I won't rest until I have extolled the architectural details of the room we're in. If you're British, I mention dental work, if you're French, I'll bring up World War II. If you hail from Colombia, I'll blurt out something about drug trafficking; Swedish people get to hear about their suicide rates. If you're Canadian, I'll just stand there in stupefied silence because I can't think of something inappropriate about Canada, and that leaves me with nothing to say.

I wasn't always like this. When I was a small child, I had no problem chatting with anyone. Since most children are usually asked things like "How old are you?" and "Do you want another slice of cake?" I experienced only smooth sailing when it came to small talk. I was no Gore Vidal but I could hold up my end of a conversation. So what caused things to go so terribly wrong for me? Journalists, that's what.

The first interview I ever did was right before *The Goodbye Girl* started shooting. Three actors, one director, and about a hundred reporters staring at us like we were the new panda exhibit at the zoo. I have no recollection of the question that was asked of me, but I do remember my answer: "I'm very lucky. I don't have a stage-struck family and a pushy mother."

It wasn't a long answer. I didn't mumble. My voice carries across a room even when I whisper. So you can imagine my surprise when I saw the quote in the paper the next day:

"I have a stage-struck family and a pushy mother."

True, he only missed one word, but it was kind of an important one. That one word might have been the difference between a reasonably normal childhood and Quinn, two years later, hoovering lines of Bolivian flake off the belly of a bartender at Studio 54. Even a nine-year-old knew that statement didn't reflect well upon my family. I cried. I flung the paper around my room and then around the house. My mother threw it away. I retrieved it from the trash and flung it around some more. Finally, after long periods of comforting me and stepping over flung paper, my mother sat me down. "Quinn, it's over," she said. "He made a mistake. I know you didn't say that. Papa knows you didn't say that. It was one line in a small article, and it won't happen again."

Some of what my mother said was true. The event had taken place in the past and therefore, in the strictest sense of the word, met the definition of "over." My parents knew I hadn't said that, and they were all that really mattered. It was one line in a small article. The part that might not have been true—that the reporter made an honest mistake transcribing my taped words—is between the reporter and his god (and the paper's ombudsman). But the part where my mother said it would never happen again was pure wishful thinking.

During the publicity push for the movie, I estimate I did five hundred interviews and there was a misquote in about four hundred of them. Mostly, they were benign. The cat was named "Pooh," not "Winnie." I grew up in West Hollywood, not Hollywood. I had never indicated any great interest in *Charlie's Angels* nor had I longed to be confused with Kate Jackson. Some of these journalistic blunders could be easily traced to a lapse of objectivity—they were more about the interviewer than the interviewee. One very elderly reporter in New York talked to me for a few minutes at the post-premiere party and subsequently wrote a little piece about how I complained the music was too loud and that my feet hurt. I'm guessing her editor cut the part where I ranted about how bad Geritol tasted and that nothing good had come out of Hollywood since actors started talking. The rest just followed the tried and true journalistic traditions of taking things out of context and making shit up.

It wasn't like I did myself any great favors when given the chance to speak without an intermediary. The first talk show I ever did was *The Tonight Show with Johnny Carson*. My mother, knowing my tendency to obsess a subject into separate atoms of anxiety, had neutrally said, "Oh, that should be fun," giving it no more weight than a field trip to the planetarium. Unfortunately, everyone else in my life thought it would be best to take me aside, look deeply into my eyes, and explain in portentous tones, "This is a very big deal." Nobody actually added "So don't screw up!" At least not out loud. But, really, we all knew the fate of this interview was in my grubby hands, right next to my flayed cuticles. As the day loomed, I mutated from a pleasantly excited nine-year-old into an overcaffeinated Yorkshire terrier. Some genius told me millions of people would be watching. Had someone drawn my blood that day, it would have registered as a mixture of adrenaline and jet fuel.

The afternoon of the show, I was in the makeup room having what I would now describe as a teensy, weensy, preadolescent anxiety attack when the publicity woman breezed in. She hugged me, careful not to get too close to my lip gloss, and said warmly, "Just be yourself. Be funny. It'll be fine." What I learned within the next hour is that when I'm nervous, being told to be funny acts upon me as a Bic lighter acts upon a plume of hair spray. During the interview, I was aware of the heat of the stage lights, the thudding of my heart, and the constant yapping of some unbearably obnoxious individual with a taste for insult comedy. Gradually, I grew to suspect that the voice was mine. Anyone watching the show would have thought "My God, she's the hellspawn of Don Rickles and Joan Rivers, only less appealing. I'm taking extra birth-control measures tonight!"

I finished my segment, walked offstage, fell into my mother's arms, and cried. I cried as we walked backstage. I cried in the car. I cried as I did my homework. I cried as I scoured off the makeup. I cried and choked as I brushed my teeth. I cried as I went to sleep. What was supposed to be America's first glimpse of my real personality had only established that the title of World's Most Odious Child Ever was now a lock. I'm in no position to say whether or not under normal conditions I was a kid you'd want to spend time with, but what I had become on that night, on that show, was some weird drag-queen version of myself. And I couldn't even pretend it wasn't as bad as it was because for weeks afterward, people would approach me and say, "I saw you on Carson!" Then, realizing they had to complete the thought, would flail around a bit and add something like "Wow!" My appearance had been the talk-show version of a massive tire fire. Am I exaggerating? I was told later that Mr. Carson refused to invite children to *The Tonight Show* after my segment. It's hard not to take that personally.

In a matter of months, I learned that if I talked to other people and they wrote down my words I'd probably sound like an idiot; if I spoke for myself, I'd make people want to punch me. Now cripplingly self-conscious, whenever I was interviewed I'd blather mindless platitudes with an occasional inappropriate pronouncement thrown in for flavor.

INTERVIEWER: So, how do you like acting?

QUINN: I like acting very much. It's fun. I like to have fun. Fun is nice.

INTERVIEWER: But don't you feel as if you are missing out on your childhood?

QUINN: No, because I am having fun. Which is nice. I like fun, especially when it's nice.

INTERVIEWER: Oh . . . kay.

Agonizing silence.

QUINN: If I eat shellfish, I vomit.

After *The Goodbye Girl*, I joined a television show that had already been on the air for two years. By then, every other actor on the show had told the publicity people they'd rather perform their own hemorrhoidectomy than do another interview, which is why I was frequently drafted to talk to reporters. The problem was that entertainment reporters sent out to interview children usually bear resentment so palpable it leaves a stain on the carpet:

> I'm the entertainment reporter from the *Regional-Standard-Eagle-Picayune,* a very important paper known in the tristate area for its coverage of the weather. There are three movies coming out this weekend; I might have interviewed the hot ingénue and maybe talked her into sex. I might have interviewed the famous old British actor and gotten drunk with him and heard stories about him banging Jacqueline Bisset. But, no, I was assigned to interview a child on a TV show. If I'm not getting laid or drunk, remind me again why I took those journalism classes at community college.

This led to a string of frustrated reporters hoping and praying for me to say something—anything—stupid and inflammatory to justify their expense report. These weren't the most subtle of predators. Oddly enough, many of them were named Skip.

In most of these interviews I'd be sitting on my couch at home, while my mother was sitting nearby.

SKIP: So . . . you have a dog?

QUINN: Yeah. This one.

Quinn points to the dog that has crawled on the couch between them.

SKIP: Okay, yeah. And you like dogs?
QUINN: Sure.

The phone rings. Quinn's mother leaves the room to answer it.
The reporter waits until he can hear her on the phone,
leans in over the dog, and speaks quickly.

SKIP: How much money do you make?
QUINN: I don't know.
SKIP: Of course you do. What do you make a week?
QUINN: My mom hasn't told me.

In fact, she hadn't. Brilliantly sensing it would prevent me from ever having to lie or accidentally slipping up, she didn't tell me until I was eighteen. This added to Skip's frustration.

SKIP: This is a nice house. Do you parents spend all your
    money? I bet your parents spend all your money.
QUINN: Of course they don't.
SKIP: If you don't know how much money you make, how
    do you know they're not spending it?
QUINN: I . . . they wouldn't do that.
SKIP: God, you're so naïve. I have an idea. Let's take a look
    at your mother's checkbook. If she's innocent, there's no
    harm in that, right? Where's her checkbook?

Then there were the reporters who would keep rephrasing the question until I gave them something not entirely unlike what they were already planning to write:

SKIP: You work with Kristy McNichol.

QUINN: Yes.

We both wait for something to occur to one of us.

SKIP: Bet that's hard. *She's* so famous and loved by
     everyone and you're . . . well, you know. Everyone
     loves *her.* You're jealous, right?

QUINN: No.

SKIP: So, who is your favorite on the set?

QUINN: I like everyone. Sada Thompson gave me this great
     book about . . .

SKIP: But not Kristy, right? Sibling rivalry. It's natural.

QUINN: We're not really sisters.

SKIP: Of course you're not. Just let it out.

See the article the next day. See the publicity picture of me
the paper chose to use. Note how I am scowling. The caption
underneath says, in big block letters, "KRISTY IS NO SIS-
TER OF MINE!" See me apologizing to Kristy for the impression the reporter has given that I have a secret voodoo altar with
black candles, Kristy McNichol dolls, and a few dozen well-
placed pins.

Not every reporter was setting traps and snare pits into our
conversations. If two out of the five resented my very existence,
another two were irrationally proud of their ability to talk to
children. *I love children!* they'd think. *My nephew is a child.
He's . . . what is he now? Four? No, he just went to college so
that makes him . . . fifteen? Something like that.* Armed with
almost a total lack of experience talking to anyone who didn't

live through the Cuban Missile Crisis, they'd arrive and we'd enjoy a conversation that whipsawed between *Romper Room* and *Meet the Press*. Skip would ask me if I liked dollies. If I mentioned that I wasn't so interested in dolls—being eleven and all—he'd ask me what I thought the Fed was going to do in response to the inflation rate.

The bulk of my interviews occurred between the ages of nine and eleven. That's less than one-thirteenth of my life. I've spent more time trying to grow out a bad perm. Yet I never really considered how spending three formative years being asked intrusive questions by aggressive, microphone-wielding strangers might possibly damage one's brain. In my teens, I was frozen with self-loathing and self-consciousness, but John Hughes movies taught me we all felt that way, and he was right. John Hughes movies also convinced me I could wear a short, bright-red bob and mismatched used clothing and not look like someone's grandmother in Boca Raton. In that case, he was mistaken.

In my twenties, I assumed that my conversational problem had something to do with meeting people at parties, which meant I was already two or three glasses into something delightful mixed with tonic. And if you mix it like this . . .

GIN (or) VODKA (and) Lime (and) Tonic

. . . you say many things that don't measure up to the usual requirements for polite social intercourse. But there was no Bosworth noting all of my idiotic and inflammatory ramblings since the smartest of my friends were usually vomiting into a hedge.

In time, I outgrew my need to be the short girl who could keep up, drink for drink, with the tall boys. I also got a job as a talent agent—a career choice that didn't improve my conversational skills in any meaningful way, but no one seemed to notice. If the bulk of the people with whom you are communicating are actors, it's safe to say you aren't doing a lot of the talking. A few more years went by and I found myself pregnant. Once again, I was a dreadful conversationalist, but this time I could blame hormones. For the entire pregnancy all I wanted to do was sleep, smile off into space, or find another woman in the room who either was pregnant or had been pregnant at some point, with whom I could compare bizarre symptoms. It's really the last time until retirement age when a person can discuss bladder control with a stranger in a public space.

Then Alice was born and she turned out to be one of those children who only slept for minutes at a stretch. She was delightful and I was happy, but I was also getting by on ninety minutes of sleep a day, sometimes while driving. No one at a social gathering ever confused me for Oscar Wilde or Dorothy Parker. If I determined the person standing next to me had children, I would begin quizzing them about wait-lists at local preschools. If they didn't have children, I would rack my brains for a conversation starter.

We weren't going anywhere on vacation, I wasn't reading any books not dedicated to fostering good eating habits for preschoolers, and I kept insisting Julianne Moore was in every movie I saw so pop culture was out of the question as conversation fuel. If witty conversation is a garden, I was the strip of dirt between the dog run and the easement. But this will pass, I kept telling myself as I rummaged through my purse scrounging desperately for something to talk about. I will get one good night's sleep and I will rise up the next day as the sparkling conversationalist I hallucinated I had once been.

Years have passed. I sleep now. I occasionally read a book. I know that while Julianne Moore does many movies, she isn't in every single movie I see and sometimes I mean Laura Linney and sometimes I mean Liev Schreiber. And still, I make an ass out of myself at least twice a day. Alice and I attended a Chinese New Year festival in Chinatown. There were, conservatively, a billion people crammed into a two-block radius, all of them shouting. Firecrackers were going off. On the streets, people had given up driving and were reduced to leaning on their horns in some desperate attempt to create a travel wormhole by irritating the universe.

A large family passed by and, in the thick flow of pedestrian traffic, somehow appropriated Alice, her small frame getting swallowed up in the multigenerational wave of Chinese people eager to buy fish. Sensing an adventure, she threw herself into a crevice between a grandmother and a couple of teenagers. What I thought was: *Daughter of mine, do not insinuate yourself into other people's families, even if they are buying live fish, which, let me assure you, are not anticipating a long life of beloved pethood. Come back to your mother, flawed though she may be, and she will love you deeply and buy you sesame noodles.*

That's what I thought. What actually came out of my mouth?

Alice, get back here! These aren't our people!

So quiet. No firecrackers. No horns. No one shouting in any language. Not even a cracked knuckle. Only my voice, pitched for clarity and distance, ringing with insensitivity and prejudice all the way past Chinatown, through Little Tokyo, into Korea-town, and halfway across Lesser Armenia. Grimly, I took Alice's hand and said, "Come on, sweetie. It's time to go. Mommy needs to start dinner and sever her vocal cords." Silently, we headed home.

A Nice Big Fat One

I AWOKE TO THE SOUND OF OUR DOG RUPERT MAKING A spectacle of himself, burrowing under the Bench of Random Objects, an Indonesian settee that had been placed temporarily in the bedroom ten years ago. Unless he'd developed a sudden fascination with folded sweaters, extension cords, and back issues of *The New Yorker*, I couldn't imagine what the charm might be. I lay in bed, focused my eyes, and watched. Rupert wasn't interested in the bench as much as the rear leg, nearest the hamper. He threw his butt in the air and tried repeatedly to reach something with his paw. I assumed he had somehow tossed his beloved stuffed lizard behind the furniture, and I knew neither of us would rest until he retrieved it. We hadn't had him long, but I already knew that Rupert was hugely—some might say unnaturally—devoted to his toys.

I got out of bed and crouched down to recover the prize. I squinted in the shadows. It wasn't a stuffed blue lizard. When did we get him a stuffed mouse? An incredibly realistic stuffed mouse? An uncannily realistic simulacrum of a mouse?

"Oh, eeew," I moaned, still fixated on the little gray corpse. The dog thumped his tail. "Yes!" he seemed to be saying. "Oh wondrous day! An object that is small enough to carry around and also smells intoxicatingly of death. Please pull it out and we can take turns holding it in our mouths." Lulabelle the cat was nowhere nearby, but I recognized her handiwork. God knows, I've seen enough of it.

My life as coroner for the tiny began several years ago. Consort had taken Alice out for a daddy and daughter date, which can also be translated as "Daddy wants pizza." Taking good care of myself during child-free moments in the way the parenting magazines suggest, I stood over the sink having a cheese sandwich and a glass of wine. (Please pick up my book, *Elegant Dining for One,* when it's published later this year.) I finished my sandwich and stood for a second, trying to decide if a cheese sandwich over the sink was charming and bohemian, but a cheese sandwich over the sink followed by a Popsicle over the sink was just sad. That's when I noticed that even though I had finished eating I still heard chewing.

After tiptoeing daintily through the kitchen in a manner honoring the lead hippo in *Fantasia*, I determined the chewing was coming from within the walls. Whatever was having its dinner in there had enough jaw strength to make a sound discernible through an eighty-year-old plaster wall and all the way across the room. Considering my options, I did what any modern, equality-seeking, home-owning woman would do: I grabbed a Popsicle and hid in the bedroom until Consort returned home.

Because I am an animal lover by nature, we began our domestic de-rodentification with Havahart traps. I am unaware of any rescue and rehabilitation shelters that specialize in vermin so I can't imagine what I thought we were going to *do* if we actually trapped any of these critters alive, but that issue never materialized. The Havahart trap turned out to be more of a

Have-a-Snack buffet for our prey. There was no morsel so sticky the critter couldn't spring it, devour it, and walk away completely unscathed, clapping the dust from its palms like a teamster. I use the term "critter" because even though Consort insisted it was a mouse, I was sure that anything I could hear flossing inside a wall was probably large enough to loan me a jacket. In order to settle this dispute, we would need to actually trap one of these buggers and that was not working out as we'd hoped. Whatever it was in there, I had come to expect a note requesting more breadsticks and a wine list.

We upgraded to the sticky traps, which seemed like a good idea until a wall-denizen actually got stuck on one. I was in bed reading myself to sleep when I suddenly heard a jujitsu tournament in the kitchen. The sound appeared to be originating from under the sink and was accompanied by squeaks of terror. This was going to be unsightly. I toyed with buying an airline ticket to the Cayman Islands and starting a new life, but chose instead to foist this on my life partner.

I found him in the garage being masculine with a chop saw and encouraged him to come into the kitchen and do something we might laugh about in thirty years. The rodent was dispatched in as swift and humane a fashion as Consort could muster. A trash bag was involved. And a shovel. We concluded that glue traps, while saving us from having to stare at rodent innards, are terribly cruel to the animal. So we moved up to the traditional snap traps of the Looney Tunes/Acme variety. These were purchased, anointed with cheese smothered in peanut butter, and hidden in places where neither the child nor the dog would discover the awesome strength of spring-loaded steel.

For a few days nothing happened. We thought maybe we had caught the lone invader in the sticky trap. The new traps remained unsprung. I was no longer hearing the symphony of gnawing in the walls. Maybe there had just been the one.

SNAP! SNAP! SNAP!

All illusions were dispelled.

In the morning, we discovered that all three traps were licked clean of food, without so much as a whisker trapped under the murderous bar.

Consort noted, "That's one incredibly smart mouse."

I thought, *That would be because it's a rat*, but I held my tongue. Consort's Achilles' heel seemed to be the idea of sharing a house with a rat, however temporarily. As long as I pretended we were hosting the Albert Einstein of mice, Consort wouldn't sleep in his car.

The next night, we set the traps with extra-tempting, extra-aromatic peanut butter and went to bed. Consort and I were reading when I heard something from the laundry room.

I whispered, "Do you hear that?"

Consort listened for a second.

"I don't hear anything," he said and went back to his magazine.

I waited a second and heard it again.

Footsteps. Heavy footsteps.

The swish of a hairless tail.

"Ugh, it's in the back room," I shrieked, but softly. I don't know why I kept my voice down. I certainly wasn't concerned that my words might make the rat self-conscious.

Consort sat up and said in his best humor-the-woman-I-love tone, "It's not in the back room."

I hissed, "Just go look. Please. I'll wait here."

[Readers, please note my behavior here: I heard noises and hid in the bedroom, I called Consort in rather than take care of a trapped mouse, and now I'd sent him into the laundry room because I thought I heard something. All I needed was a frilly apron and a prize-winning cake recipe using Miracle Whip and I could make the cover of the April 1955 edition of *Ladies' Home Journal*.]

Consort sighed noisily and shuffled toward the back room, muttering the whole way.

" 'Read those *New Yorkers*,' she says. 'Please get them out of the house,' she says. So, I finally sit down to get through some of them and what does she do? She has me hunting for imaginary . . . OH. MY. GOD!"

The next few minutes were a frightening series of grunts, rapid footsteps, and things being overturned. I stood at the kitchen doorway, too alarmed to come closer. I heard the back door open and close. Consort staggered out of the laundry room, sweating. He looked at me in disbelief.

"It threw a bottle of bleach at me."

"Is it still back there?"

Consort nodded and said, "I tried to herd it out the back door, but it went behind the dryer and now I can't see it."

Consort and I stepped hesitantly into the laundry room. Everything but the washer and the dryer had been upended. I stood guard with a broom while Consort gingerly slid the dryer away from the wall. There was no rat. There was, however, a hole about the diameter of a quarter, under the dryer's exhaust vent. We looked at each other.

"Could it have gone through there?"

Consort shook his head. "You didn't see how big this thing was. It was wearing my shoes. There is no way it got through that hole."

But apparently it could, and did, go through the hole. The exterminator we called the next day took no small delight in telling us that rats can basically make themselves flat enough to pass through a soda straw and that our old house was laden with rat-friendly highways and shortcuts. I pictured a verminous version of Chutes and Ladders. Wherever we set a trap, our houseguests would simply find another route. Our rats had traffic options Los Angeles commuters could only fantasize about. Also, they can breed up to five times a year and produce up to fourteen pups per litter. We were, in a word, screwed.

So, starting that very day, Steve the Rat Guy would appear once or twice a week and remove three or four little casualties from his arsenal of industrial-strength traps. I liked Steve. He was punctual, he was efficient, and while he wasn't cheap he made up for it by his professional demeanor. He would enter the house. He would go to the traps. There would be a few minutes of quiet and then he would leave with a few small, opaque black bags, tied together and hanging across his chest. At another period of my life I might have been inclined to put this behavior into the category of "odd" as opposed to "soothing," but those little bags meant my vermin problem could remain a wonderfully abstract concept. I no longer had to contemplate how something that spread the Black Death and killed one-third of Europe's population was now frolicking in our walls.

One week, Steve the Rat Guy sent in his place Mike the Rat-Guy-in-Training. Mike the Rat-Guy-in-Training operated under the assumption that if people were paying you to do a job, they wanted to hear all about it. He went to check a trap and hollered back, "Nice big fat one!" He went to the next trap, poked his head into the living room where I sat, and asked, "You didn't happen to find a rat with only two legs around here, did you?" In the laundry room, he reached under the washer, pulled out a trap, and peered at it thoughtfully. Holding the trap out to me he said questioningly, "It's either a really big mouse or a baby rat. What do you think?" Choosing not to play Guess the Vermin with a pro, I fled to the bedroom with then-baby Alice. A few minutes later there was a knock at the door. Mike was apologetic. It seems that while he was up in the crawl space over Alice's room he accidentally kicked something that fell down the hatch opening and into her closet. He cleaned up most of it and, he added proudly, at least we now knew where the other half of that rat went. Steve returned the following week, his understated bandoleer of doom a welcome sight.

At about the time we decided to list Steve the Rat Guy as a dependent for tax purposes, I got a call from a friend who lived around the corner. Her family's housing situation had changed abruptly and they were desperately looking for a new place to live. Finding rental housing with a dog was complicated; finding it with a dog, a cat, and proximity to her daughter's school was nearly impossible. The only house they found was on a major thoroughfare, pretty much assuring a quick and nasty demise for their tough, beloved little street cat. She had a request.

I walked into the office where Consort was scowling at a spreadsheet and mumbling incantations. I announced, in what I hoped was a *whee!-aren't-we-spontaneous-people!* kind of way, "Long story short, we're getting a cat."

Yanked from a place where things made logical sense back into the world where I forced him to live, Consort absorbed this new information. "If I ask for the longer story, is there any way I could talk you out of this?"

I kissed him sweetly and said, "No."

Lulabelle arrived the next morning. Her owner, my about-to-move friend, was smiling in relief and sniffling in sadness. Lulabelle was scowling. We let her out of the cat carrier and into the living room where she paused just long enough to whap our then-dog Polly on the nose, then flew twice around the room in search of an exit. She fled into the bedroom and darted under the dresser where she sulked for two days. When she finally did leave her sanctuary, it was to scamper out the back door and return to her old house where, minutes later, I found her curled up on the front porch waiting to be let in. For the next few weeks, her to-do list read:

#1. Flee.

#2. Wait at old house for real owners who are taking an unaccountably long time at the grocery store.

#3. Be kidnapped by Horrible Stranger who takes you to new house with canine idiot.

#4. Eat Horrible Stranger's kitty stars while plotting the next day's escape. Fill time by taunting canine idiot.

#5. See 1.

After about three weeks, I went to the back door to invite Lulabelle inside as I had done every night since she'd arrived. I had no realistic hope she would be out there. I was about to get my coat to make the trip around the corner when I noticed a sharp glittery light out in the darkness of the yard. It was the illumination from the laundry room window reflecting back from Lulabelle's yellow eyes.

She was lying on the ground. Something about half her length was trapped under her paws struggling desperately to get away. Lulabelle glanced down for a second, put her paw firmly on its head, and glanced up at me as if to say, "Is this urgent? I'm a little booked up right now."

I shut the door delicately and waited. If this kept up, maybe we could create a system: a sock on the doorknob meant she was in the middle of preparing dinner and expected a little privacy. A half-hour later, I opened the door and the whiskered angel of death slithered in, feeling especially good about life. She sauntered to our bedroom, jumped on the Bench of Random Objects, curled up between a stapler and a Christmas wreath, and slept the sleep of the just until well into the next morning.

In the years since then, we came to learn that not only is Lulabelle an excellent ratter and mouser, she is a superlative birder, a more than competent squirreler, and probably a talented destroyer of untended Chihuahuas. Anything weighing less than five pounds with the poor luck to rest on the ground even briefly is a potential entree. Out of some feline sense of honor, Lulabelle usually tithes tails, wings, and heads to me, her landlord of record. I measure the advent of spring not with the first crocus but the first bird skull. I long to explain to Lu that we only wanted the ugly and verminous eaten, but that would have been like asking Godzilla to stomp only Tokyo's less popular neighborhoods. I attached a little bell to her collar but the body count didn't seem to diminish. The only noticeable effect was that for scores of small creatures in the vicinity of our yard, their last thought was: *Say, what's the odd ring—*

If I could keep her inside forever, I would. But that would involve none of the rest of the family ever opening a door or a window, not even for a second. Eventually, we must buy groceries or sign for a package and Lady Death will slip through any open portals relentless and stealthy as a Mossad enforcer. In truth, were we to never open the door, I'm convinced she would amuse herself by killing and eating us . . . When I hear about domesticated cats being introduced to Australia and decimating local populations of birds and small mammals, I imagine maybe five or six of Lulabelle's cousins methodically stalking an entire continent, eradicating anything smaller than a mature wallaby.

Rupert and I stared at the tiny dead mouse under the Bench of Random Objects. Not wanting to play mouse corpse tug-of-war with the dog, I shoveled the little carcass onto a shirt cardboard and carefully walked it through the house toward the trash bins outside, Rupert prancing at my heels the whole time. Crossing the dining room, I noticed Lulabelle curled up asleep on a chair—a benign vision of shiny fur and plump, pettable rump. The night before, she had allowed Alice to dress her in doll clothing. Rupert continued to angle for the new chew toy in the cardboard dustpan. I sharply commanded him to "Leave it" and he looked abashed. In the end, I thought, dogs are domesticated, cats are appeased. I stopped for a second to enjoy Lulabelle's peaceful aura, her sweet sleeping silhouette. Then I dumped her rent check in the trash bin.

In the Criminal Justice System

IF YOU HAVE RUN OUT OF REASONS TO BE GRATEFUL IN
your life, try being grateful that I am not currently trying to
help you. I am very bad at helping.

I was dropping Alice off at school one morning when I mentioned to my friend Veronica that I was heading to a nearby
neighborhood to buy a particular kind of embroidery thread.
My destination was a sweet, bucolic little village that managed
to retain its midcentury charm while Los Angeles sprawled
around it like a rash. Let's call it Mayberry.

"Oh, I love Mayberry," Veronica said. "I have to go down
there at some point this week and put up fliers for my son's soccer team pancake breakfast fund-raiser."

"Do *you* have to do it, or does it just have to get done?"

"It just has to get done, I guess."

My heart swelled. I could be helpful! "Let me do it. I'm going there anyway."

Veronica looked pleased but doubtful. "Are you sure? You'd
just have to put a few up in the coffee shop and the bookstore,
but it's still a hassle."

"It's nothing, I'll be there anyway," I said, and hugged her in a
way to indicate I live to do pancake-based errands. "Put a flier in
the coffee shop. Put a flier in the bookstore. *How hard can it* be?"

Yeah, I said this out loud. I think the universe might have
actually soiled itself laughing.

If I had done only what she asked me to do, it would have been just that easy. Everything started out so well. I found street parking with money left on the meter; that always puts me in a good mood. The employees at the local coffeehouse motioned me toward a cork board over which was a handwritten sign that read "Neighborhood Events." How easy could this be?

I love Mayberry for many reasons, but one of them is that the people here liked 1962 so much they never actually left it. There is a nonchain pet store. There is a nonchain family-owned book-store. The bank is part of a chain but it's a relatively small chain and they hand out candy at Halloween. The main street has a sewing-machine repair shop, for heaven's sake. I might be alarmed by sewing machines but I'm charmed that people out there still use them enough to require a repair shop. When I walk around this village all I want is a pillbox hat and a purse that snaps closed. Not surprisingly, they also have a needlework store, which is why I had come here to begin with. I got my embroidery thread and I tacked up another pancake flier. I was so pleased with my general goodness that I might have beatified myself, if such a thing were possible. That's when I noticed a tiny ballet studio across the street.

You know, I thought virtuously, *I'll go that one extra step and put a flier in the ballet studio. Mothers sit in ballet hallways for hours, some of them are sure to want to support a local soccer team by eating carbohydrates.*

Glowing with the blended sensation of accomplishment and errand-combining, I trotted across the street and approached the front door. The lights inside were off but the door was un-locked. I stepped inside.

"Hello?" I warbled.

There was no response.

I walked farther down the dark hallway, figuring someone was teaching a class in the back studio. I located the reception desk and saw no one. A cool breeze swept up my spine. It occurred to me that either someone had forgotten to lock up the night before or I was about to become the first scene in an episode of *Law & Order*. At best, I'd be the innocent bystander who discovers the tutu-clad corpse; at worst I'd be the innocent bystander, strangled by toe-shoe ribbons, who is later described by the detective as "dying for a career break." Either way, I decided that outside the building was a good place to be.

[Let it be noted that before I left, I carefully tacked a flier to the bulletin board.]

Back outside, I weighed my options. There was no emergency number on the door and no security system to call. I walked into the lingerie store next door. In keeping with the general tone of the block, this was not a shop packed with ribbony bits of silk underwear hinting at depravity. It was the place that answered the question: "Where can I possibly get a huge pointy-cupped bra and a holiday-themed housecoat?" I asked if they had a contact number for the dance studio. They did not. They did, however, tell me that there was a police annex just around the corner.

Police annex? Doesn't "annex" mean extra bit? This is an extra bit of a police station? Like a third nipple? That couldn't be right. Here in Mayberry "annex" probably meant small yet perfectly formed offices filled with clean-cut young people eager to walk into dark buildings. I walked briskly over to the police station, which not only wasn't a station, it wasn't even big enough to count as an annex. If it ate a lot of protein and got enough sleep, it might grow into an annex. Right now, it was a deep closet, a place where you could pay a meter ticket or get fingerprints done for security reasons. Still, it was an official police station. I got to the door and noted a sign that read: "Open from 11:00 a.m. to 3:00 p.m." I tried the door; it was locked. I checked my watch; it was 1:00 p.m. I knocked a few times and waited to see if Deputy Fife would emerge from the back room rubbing his eyes, but no luck. I'd have taken Otis the Town Drunk by this point. I walked into the shoe repair place next door. The cobbler smiled welcomingly.

I gestured to the wall he shared with the police.

"Do you know why the office might be closed?"

He thought.

"Sometimes, if it's quiet, they don't come in."

I guessed the local hooligans, whippersnappers, and roust-abouts must have been in the pokey. I walked back to the ballet studio and paced outside a few more minutes, then determined that calling 911 was in order. I was promptly routed to a phone system that asked me to "Press one if this is an emergency." Standing there on the street, I faced one of my civic conundra. Was this an emergency? Was arterial blood clotting on the sprung floor six yards away from where I dithered? I didn't know. Was it *not* an emergency? Did I want to be one of those people who clog up the 911 system with calls complaining about how the neighbor is stealing my newspaper again?

I did not. I just wanted someone to walk into this dark build-ing who wasn't me.

I didn't press 1 and waited in the silence.

I walked back to the bookstore while I waited and bought a cup of tea. After five minutes or so, I checked my cell phone. I had been disconnected. I redialed 911 and again I didn't press 1. But this time, being familiar with the subtleties of the 911 hold signal, I kept an eye on the readout. Almost instantly, I had been disconnected again. Apparently, admitting you weren't trying to remove an icepick from your own sternum meant the 911 system kind of wanted you to go away.

I called 911 again. This time, I pressed 1.

I waited.

I waited.

I waited. The silence was piercing. On 911, no one thanks you for your patience or lets you know that you'll be taken in the order received. No one ever even hinted our call might be monitored for quality assurance. I guess when your life is unpleasant enough to require a call to 911, you just want to take it for granted that everyone knows what they're doing.

I checked the phone; I was still technically on hold, which was something like an improvement from before. For fun, I checked my watch; I had walked in the ballet studio twenty-five minutes ago. All I wanted to do was run away, but of course I couldn't, because no one else seemed to know this stupid door was open, and there was still a chance that some innocent ballerina was being defiled with a leg warmer, and *would no one pick up my emergency call?*

It was at that moment that I saw a police car head down the street. Finally, a good guy with a gun! I raced after the police car, yelling like some sort of deranged do-gooder, spilling tea all over myself, saturating the one flier I had left, and managing somehow to disconnect myself from 911.

Of course, the police car sailed on, and disappeared. But at least I had a new piece of information. The police car had the name of a nearby city. Mayberry's peace and stability were the responsibility of an adjacent municipality. All it took was one call to information, and I was connected to that city's police department.

And put on hold.

I waited.

I waited.

I waited.

I was disconnected.

Of course, between holding the dregs of my tea, my cell phone, and the pulpy mass that was the last flier, I hadn't actually written down the number so I had to call 411 again. They put me through.

I waited.

I waited.

I . . . wait, I got someone!

I gabbled in relief, "Hi, I'm standing on a street and I walked into a building, which shouldn't be open but it was, and it was dark, and I think maybe someone didn't lock it last night, or maybe there's been a crime, and who wants to be the person in the first scene of *Law & Order*, right? Anyway . . ."

"Where are you located, ma'am?"

I told her.

"That's not our jurisdiction, ma'am."

I spluttered, "But I just saw one of your cars drive past here!"

She waited that extra second, which lets the speaker know she's said something stupid.

"Ma'am, I can't tell why the police car was there. Maybe they were going to lunch. It's not our jurisdiction."

"Then whose jurisdiction *is* it?"

She told me. I called. I was placed on hold. Ten minutes later a dispatcher got on the line.

"Hi," I said dully. "I'm in front of a building that is unlocked, and probably shouldn't be. Could you please fix it?"

She asked the address. I told her, and held my breath.

"Can you wait for the police officer?"

"Hell yes, I can wait!" I crowed happily.

I had reached that magical stage in my helpfulness ritual where I slid so far into a secondary problem that I had completely forgotten the original task. As far as I could remember, I had been born on this corner waiting for someone to arrive and walk into a dark building. The police officer appeared a few minutes later. He was reassuringly big.

I explained: Dark building . . . nobody inside . . . came right back out . . . called for help.

"Yeah," he said, matter-of-factly. "You don't want to be the person who finds the body, like on *Law & Order*."

I swear, I heard angels singing.

And the Livin' Is Easy

I HAVE READ ABOUT EVERY CAMP OPTION IN SOUTHERN California, and I've noticed a couple of patterns. First of all, the people who write camp brochures are crazy for exclamation points! It's as if they worry we might not understand how much fun their camp is unless they're shouting at us! Really! Second, I'm convinced they are all using the same picture of the same three children, carefully chosen for diversity and attractiveness, smiling blissfully and holding up a frog. It could be a hiking in the Sierras camp or computer camp in the basement of the local vocational school, but it's the same three kids and that same damned frog.

And there are so very many camps. At first, I was swamped and humbled by all the wonderful and enriching ways that Alice could spend the summer. Seventy or so brochures later, I noticed they had other things in common besides that damned frog. There were definite types. In case you haven't gotten around to finding the right camp yet, here are some of your options:

• CAMP UTOPIA: Now in our seventy-fifth year, Camp Utopia provides the ideal environment for children to grow into young adults and future leaders. Our activities include archery, horseback riding, swimming in our very own lake, toasting marshmallows while singing under a starry sky, and making memories to last a lifetime!

Some former campers have called Utopia "The finest hours of my childhood" and "The place that taught me how to be a person of honor and integrity." All of our camp counselors have a Master's degree in Childhood Development, and our Camp Leader, Mr. Robby, received a Presidential Commendation for his work with children!

Camp Utopia is currently accepting wait-list applications for the week of August 20–24, 2017. Siblings and children of former Utopians and U.S. senators will receive first priority.

• CAMP ACADEMIA: It's summertime, and the living is easy . . . for losers! Here at Camp Academia we know that a month not spent boning up on standardized testing skills is a month other kids leap ahead of your child. We will make sure your five- to thirteen-year-old spends a productive day memorizing prime numbers, practicing their Chinese vocabulary, crafting the perfect essay, and boning up on the periodic table!

But it's not all #2 pencils here at Camp Academia! Each afternoon, campers have an hour of *Yoga for Stress Management and Excellence!* Our cafeteria serves only high-Omega 3, 6, and 9 foods! And each week ends with a camp-wide game of Junior Jeopardy. Camp tradition says the first child eliminated has to wear a T-shirt printed with "I'm on my way to community college." Our kids are wise *and* wacky!

Camp Academia has a few spots left for the most motivated students. Please note on the application whether your child is prone to nervous tics, uncontrolled weeping, or stress-related skin conditions.

• CAMP EXHAUSTIA: Does the thought of having the kids around the house all summer make you crazy? Let us help! From nine to three every day, our campers run up and down a sand dune carrying heavy weights. At lunchtime, we challenge campers to eat their lunches while doing push-ups: good exercise and good coordination!

For a small fee, we have before-camp and after-camp programs where your child will learn teamwork by helping excavate a new swimming pool for the campgrounds, or building electric transmission towers . . . all by hand! If you think your child needs even more goal-oriented physical activity, this summer we are offering a special program: *Camp Persona Non Grata*, where we pick up your child directly from his last day of school and take him to work on a logging operation in Oregon until the Sunday before Labor Day. Our lucky campers spend all day, every day, in the forest, hauling cut trees over to our very own sawmill. Mother Nature meets noisy machinery! The kids have a ball!

For a small *additional* fee, we can keep your busy beaver right through the Labor Day weekend and deposit him directly into the first day of school.

When applying, please attach a copy of the child's Ritalin prescription (we like to pair roommates of similar dosages).

• CAMP DIVA: Does your six-year-old demand *Turandot* on the way to school? Does your fifth-grade son feel left out when no one wants to go with him to the Kirov Ballet? Camp Diva is a loving, nurturing environment for the artistic temperament, ages five to thirteen. No class begins before 10:00 a.m., and we always have fresh espresso ready! We offer such classes as *The Oeuvre of Harvey Fierstein*, *Sondheim for Second-Graders*, and *Tantrum as Performance Art*.

This year we will be doing a full production of *Rent*, with our returning camper Brian Abromowitz starring in the role of Mimi. But new campers needn't fret, because we're going to need lots of great singers and actors to play colorful junkies and homeless people!

We offer food options for vegetarians, vegans, lactose-intolerant, glucose-sensitive, and the recovering eating-disordered.

Please include a portfolio of your child's work along with your application. Videotapes will be acceptable for dancers, actors, and singers, but please also include recent reviews.

After weighing all the options, here is the camp Alice *will* be attending:

• CAMP CASA: For nearly a decade, Camp Casa has been giving one very special child the kind of one-on-one attention she just won't get anywhere else. She'll feel a sense of accomplishment when she empties the dryer for the very first time. She'll learn science by classifying all the spiders she finds in her backyard playhouse. She'll take private cooking lessons and learn the traditional Camp Casa breakfast: *Cereal-eaten-without-needing-to-wake-up-Mother*.

Afternoon field trips will include the beach (for no additional fee, she will learn to operate a Dustbuster and remove sand from the backseat), the park, the museum, her Aunt and Uncle's pool, and Trader Joe's.

Yeah, right. The reality is, every year I plan for a summer of mellow and inexpensive pleasures. And every year I lose my mind. The best way to describe my parenting skills is to use the model of comic improvisation. When doing comic improv there are a couple of hard and fast rules. If your improv partner walks in and says, "I'm your brother, home from an expedition to Australia where I was artificially inseminating koalas!" you can't say, "No, you aren't," because that brings the improv to a screeching halt. It also makes the other actors onstage want to spit into your latte afterward. No, you must say, "Yes, and as I recall, you're also a world-class opera singer." You always say, "Yes, *and* . . ." The "and" is everything. The "and" keeps the story going. You add the opera part because most improv people live to ad-lib an opera about extracting koala semen. My whole life is a function of "Yes, *and* . . .":

Can I carry my purse, the cat carrier, the library books, and a bag of dry-cleaning to the car? Yes, *and* I can carry a tray of cupcakes for Alice's class *and* I can hold between my teeth the bag of live crickets for the class turtle.

Can I hike twelve miles? Yes *and* I can wear my iPod so I can listen to a series of lectures on the rulers of Byzantium *and* I can page through a back issue of *Foyer* magazine, leading to confusion when I later insist the Empress Theodosia was known for her fondness for recessed lighting.

Can I make sure my daughter has some pure, uncompli-cated, relaxing down-time during her summer vacation?

Yes.

And then I hear from a mom friend about a week-long science camp where the kids explore the chemistry behind cosmetics, and who would deny her makeup-fixated daughter the chance to discover the atomic weight of lip gloss? With any luck, Alice will fall in love with chemistry and be distracted from what seems like her inevitable path toward a lifetime behind the counter at Bobbi Brown. Don't get me wrong; if learning the fifty-eight different names for lipsticks, which could all be described as "pinkish-brown," is her vocational destiny then I will wish her well. But wouldn't she make an even better saleswoman if she could pronounce all the ingredients? Also, the camp is cheap.

And then her swim coach offers a week's intensive swimming camp and happens to mention she's using a pool only three blocks from the science camp, which is good because the swimming camp starts twenty minutes after makeup camp ends. Alice loves swimming. I love when Alice is tired. Also, her most agreeable friend is going. Also, it's cheap. I quickly calculate that if I pick her up at the exact second science camp ends, scrape off the results of her morning's experiments, hand her a snack, shout at her to eat the snack for the seven minutes between destinations, teach her to change into a bathing suit in the backseat while still eating, and catapult her through the pre-swim shower room, we can make it work.

So, that's it. One week of insanity; the rest of the summer a balancing calmness.

And then we get a notice from another mom telling me she'd procured Alice a spot at her daughter's day camp. One does not just give these people money to take one's child and allow them to accumulate insect bites. No, one must be vetted by a preexisting family. Last fall, after hearing my friend's daughter gleefully describe the fun she had at day camp that summer, I offhandedly asked my friend to put us on the list. Of course, I completely forgot about it because my name is on lists all over the city for all sorts of things, and no one ever contacts me. I also forgot about the list because my brain works like an Etch A Sketch; even the slightest movement causes it to go completely blank. We were all a little surprised to hear that Alice had secured a two-week spot at the desired camp. I reread the brochure and noted the swimming, the hiking, the T-shirt tie-dyeing day, the make-your-own-pizza day, the camp Olympics day, the . . .

I felt breath on my neck. Turning around, I caught Alice reading over my shoulder. Her cheeks were flushed, her pupils were dilated. She whispered, "Please tell me I'm going there."

I had so eagerly awaited the day she started reading. That was a very long time ago.

"But," I floundered, "you're supposed to be relaxing."

She poked her finger at the brochure and said, enunciating each word, "Arts *and* Crafts *and* Karaoke day."

Fortuitously, this camp started the week after the chemistry and swimming marathon ended. This one wasn't cheap, but Grandma graciously offered to cover the cost as a birthday present.

And we were done.

And then I got a message from another mother. She had paid for both her kids to go to tennis camp and, owing to a poor decision involving a skateboard, a ramp, and several lawn chairs, her son was now the proud owner of a compound wrist fracture. She was happy to give me the other camp spot, which I wouldn't even have to pay for. She gave me the dates; tennis camp started the week after the day camp. It was a few minutes from the house. The sane voice in my head told me, "Unless Alice is part racing greyhound she will be sufficiently exercised for the summer." But the sane voice is small and timid. It was drowned out by the loud chanting, "FREE! CLOSE! FREE! CLOSE!" I borrowed tennis gear and would send her off to discover the joys of whacking at a small yellow ball while sunblock dripped into her eyes.

We were two days from the end of tennis camp and, I must admit, I was glad. Alice had had nothing short of a perfect summer so far and she was completely content with the level of campitude, but I was starting to lose perspective. There's something about packing a lunch for a child every day that drains the soul. The fact that I was trying to find the mini-bags of raisins and making sandwiches when it was over a hundred degrees outside just made me irritable and prone to lash out. We had three more weeks before school started. Alice could forage in the kitchen for food like her parents.

And then the phone rang. It was another friend with children. She had decided to run a ballet camp in her house for the following week. Dance in the morning, crafts and swimming in the afternoon. She was inviting Alice. Ignoring the voices shouting "DO IT! WE'VE GOT A HALF-TANK OF GAS AND HAND-ME-DOWN BALLET SLIPPERS!" I started to demur. I explained, "Oh, I'd love to, but Alice has been running around all summer. I think she's too worn out for ballet camp . . ."

"No, I'm not."

I put my hand over the mouthpiece of the phone and looked over my shoulder. How did my child manage to materialize out of thin air every time camp was mentioned? She bounced from foot to foot.

"I LOVE ballet camp!" she squealed in delight. I didn't doubt her sincerity but suspected that under other circumstances, she would have shrieked "I LOVE brain-eating camp!" It was Pavlovian. Alice heard the word "camp," squealed in delight, and automatically handed me my checkbook. My friend's house isn't close, but the price made up for it. On Friday, Alice was determined to be the third Williams sister, winning the French Open before she was old enough to vote. By Monday afternoon, she was certain the New York City Ballet was holding a spot for her.

Okay. Only one more week of Alice-shaped fun and Quinn-based driving.

And then a friend of a friend decided to do a three-day etiquette camp the following week. *And* then Consort found a weekend golf camp for daddies and daughters. *And* then her friend's karate instructor had an intensive beginners' course. I assumed this sudden flurry of end-of-summer camps meant any parent with a skill they could teach to other people's children had taken a look at their own bank statement.

I sat down one night in August and did the math. I, who had planned not to do any summer camp at all had already spent only slightly less on camp than I spent on Alice's school's tuition the previous year. "Yes, *and* . . ." may be fun to watch at the Comedy Store but it's toxic on your credit score. Alice came rushing up, waving a brochure.

"Look what just came in the mail," she crowed and dropped it on top of my checkbook. The day camp was thanking us for our participation this summer and reminding us that they would be doing Winter Holiday Camp from December 17 through December 31.

I whispered, "I have one more camp for you this summer."

Alice gasped in delight.

"It's called Camp Alice's Bedroom. Please go there now. I'll see you the day after Labor Day."

Kraftwerk

SO FAR, IT APPEARS I HAVEN'T FAILED AT THE MAJOR CHAL-
lenges of rearing my daughter. Alice is usually clean, she sometimes looks people in the eye, and I haven't bartered her for a
bottle of Night Train. Still, whatever pride I take in having ex-
panded the definition of adequate parenting, I have to admit I
fail at one of the more modest yet critical aspects of professional
mothering: the Making of Crafts. There are magazine racks
dedicated to every sort of project a parent and child can create
together while sitting at the kitchen table as a pot of homemade
soup bubbles on the stove. There is no holiday so obscure that a
photogenic craft can't be found somewhere to commemorate it.
Forget the obvious questions such as "Where the hell do you
put the Arbor Day tree made out of recycled neckties, paper
clips, and a shipping tube where it isn't knocking over the giant
Columbus Day faux ravioli made from a throw pillow and red
poster paint?" Let us go to the more immediate concern.

I cannot make anything that requires glue.

This problem goes back to elementary school. I remember
with terrible clarity sitting in class staring at a Valentine I had
created for my parents. It didn't resemble the traditional confec-
tion of lace and love so much as an accurate 3-D model of the
heart of a very elderly person, complete with clogged arteries
and tissue necrosis. My entire catalog of school artwork could
best be described as "unsettling" or "a cry for help." It bothers

me to think about how many trees lost their lives so I could create something that would lead teachers to say things like "Well, Rome wasn't built in a day . . ." while patting my slumped shoulder sympathetically. If there had been a class called Remedial Crafts, I would have been there stringing macaroni jewelry well into high school. Lucky for me, eventually people stop caring if you can create appealing wrapping paper using poster paint and a carved potato so I assumed I could move on with life and be incompetent in new directions.

Flash forward a couple of decades. Alice took a class on California's history at the local museum. Since the children were between three and four years old, this was mainly an excuse for the parents to get out of the house while their children ate Pepperidge Farm goldfish crackers in an educational environment. Unfortunately, the (obviously childless) person who devised the class decided it would be nice to have the children make Conestoga wagons out of shoe boxes, construction paper, pipe cleaners, and glue.

The children did exactly what was expected of them: they wandered off to eat little fish crackers and try to remove one another's eyes with pipe cleaners. The mothers were left to create whatever tangible keepsakes might justify the money we'd shelled out for the class. If I had been handed a person suffering a gunshot wound and told to stitch him up, I couldn't have been any more anxious, ill-equipped, or under-qualified. But I tried.

I cut. I glued. I attached tiny wheels made from toilet paper rolls. In total candor, it did end up resembling one of the covered wagons our pioneer forefathers used to travel across this great land. Unfortunately, it resembled the wagon after an especially ghastly migration where the native people threw rocks at it, shot it with flaming arrows, and stomped on what was left. If you looked at my wagon you would have sworn you could hear tiny pioneers sobbing from within. I shifted the remains into a paper bag and furtively bore it home. Later, Consort found the Bag of Shame and asked Alice about the class. "That's mine!" she said brightly. For a preschooler, it was some fine work.

I didn't correct her.

The years passed. Alice learned how to use scissors deftly. I learned to sense when the silence from the other room meant the scissors had left her paper and were now being used on her sheets. Her artwork improved. My ability to open a juice box with my knees and incisors while driving improved. She achieved legible printing and then handwriting. I finally learned to read her father's handwriting, a dazzling array of blots and strokes which bears a strong resemblance to Morse code in linguini. I took pride in these small glimmers of competence and clung to the delusion that Alice hadn't noticed how none of my new skills utilized a glue stick. I assumed she wasn't aware how I would start twisting my hair every time we walked near a craft store. I hoped that if I was not perfect, I was at least worthy of imitation in her eyes. And for a while, I was.

Not long ago, Alice and I were reading in perfect contentment. Or rather, I thought Alice was reading. I turned a page of my book and caught her eye as she stared thoughtfully at me. I asked why I was suddenly more interesting than those Magic Tree House kids.

"You read knitting books all the time," she said in a pensive tone. "And you're always in a good mood after you read them . . ."

Yes, I acknowledged. There's nothing like a chapter about

tightening my buttonholes to make me happy. But it seems I had interrupted her, and she continued.

". . . But you never actually knit."

Sharper than a serpent's tongue is an observant child. Now I had to confront my psychological irregularities, something I was planning to do in retirement, along with daytime drinking.

I do love to read knitting books. The pictures in knitting books leave me with nothing but happy scenes in my head:

I could make Consort and Alice these matching reindeer sweaters. They could wear them when they are playing in the snow. I could make a third matching sweater for the dog and a coordinating beanie for the cat! And a cast-cozy to go over whichever arm I injure trying to put a beanie on the cat!

I could make this blanket and drape it over the spot on the couch, just like in this picture. It will be an elegant way to cover the juice stain that didn't completely come out.

Everyone needs more pot holders.

However, actually knitting fills my head with one horrible, demoralizing question: Why does nearly everything I knit—infant cardigan, hat, sleeve—develop an uncanny resemblance to a gene sequence? The only things that don't resemble the traditional double helix are the pot holders I knit. These resemble tumors.

The secret ingredient to my freakish skill, or lack thereof, is *gauge*. For the non-knitter reading this, gauge is the number of stitches per inch to be expected from the yarn and the knitting scheme. At the beginning of any pattern, you will find a gauge guide showing how many stitches and rows it should take to create a sample size. In theory, this keeps you from creating a seventeen-foot-long sleeve. But when I see a phrase like *Gauge: 9 sts and 13 rows = 4" over Stockingette stitch* I start chewing my cuticles. I'll begin there, sure. The first three rows will be a model of conformity and balance. But I had carpal tunnel syndrome when I was pregnant and while it went slinking away within eighteen hours of my giving birth to Alice, it left me with some capricious nerve damage to my hands. I say capricious because I can type endlessly with no ill effect but if I bend my arm in the way a knitter is inclined to, within minutes the crunching inflammation comes rushing back, all too eager to remind me how it's the boss of me.

What happens is that my thumb and first three fingers go completely numb. After a couple of minutes, I can look down and watch what feels like someone else's hand knitting and purling away. If this other knitter were competent, it would actually be kind of fun. But since I have no feeling in the fingers creating the appropriate tension, I start playing something like Red Light, Green Light with the yarn. My fingers start relaxing until I could conceivably use the slackened yarn as a wee jump rope, then seeing that, I tighten up. But I tighten too much, having no digital feedback, so within a row, I have something between my fingers that looks like a garrote for a chinchilla.

In theory, a gauge sample is nearly always a square or a rectangle. When I do it, it's always Anything Can Happen Day. Once in a while, feeling naughty and rebellious, I've continued with a knitting pattern without actually confirming the gauge sample. Perhaps you already see the problem; if my hand goes numb after a few minutes and the quality of my knitting goes to hell, what happens after, say, a half hour? Terrible things. The width of the knitting drifts in, wanders out, has brief rows of consistency that only give the observer a heartbreaking glimpse of what might have been if only I knew what my fingers were doing. People looking at what I'm making tend to say the same things you say to small children who proudly present you with a picture of . . . something:

"Well, aren't you working hard!"

"You must be very proud of that!"

"Wow, Quinn, that's a great . . . That's knitting, right?"

How does it develop the iconic twisting shape of the double helix? How do I, without fail, create a shape that would be the envy of high-school biology teachers everywhere? I'm not entirely certain, but it too seems to have something to do with my numb, club-like fingers. It seems that if you are tightening and loosening the yarn at random intervals, the knitting starts to spiral, perhaps in an attempt to get away from you.

Halfway through the project, I bow to the inevitable and acknowledge that this twisted bit of increasingly arbitrary width is not going to magically transform itself into a set-in sleeve, and I unravel the yarn. I unravel the yarn sullenly. I unravel the yarn ungraciously. I unravel the yarn while picking fights with people. But I unravel the yarn. Then I commence the re-knitting of the sleeve. But it goes no better the second time around. Or the third. After the fourth time, when the yarn is now grubby and irredeemably stretched-out, I jam the entire thing into the bottom of the closet, along with the other crafting dead ends: *Anyone Can Felt* and *Decoupage for Dummies*. By the time the third half-finished double helix bounces off the closet floor, I am prepared to admit that knitting affords me no pleasure and generates no attractive accessories. In fact, knitting irritates the hell out of me.

Thinking about kniting, though, is wonderful. In my mind, I'm one of those women who knit in movie theaters. I decide on

Tuesday to whip myself up a stylish halter top and wear it on Saturday night. Alice and I pore through my most recent knitting magazine and she points to a Fair Isle sweater and shyly asks me to make it for her. I fondly pat her head and say, "Of course, sweetheart." People stop using rulers in this house, preferring to use my gauge samples, because they are *just that even*. How I love to think about knitting. When Alice came to me to learn knitting, I offered her a pile of knitting magazines and tried to teach her how to *think about* knitting. She sighed. I pretended that the problem was with knitting and my log-like fingers, not with all crafts. Surely, there were other things I could teach her to do.

Then Alice spotted a child-size sewing machine in a catalog I hadn't buried deeply enough in the recycling bin. Charmed by its size and pinkness, she declared she wanted to learn to sew. I patted her hand and said, "Well, ask for it for Christmas" in what I hoped was an "I look forward to teaching you how to sew, a thing I know how to do" tone of voice but would have more accurately been a "Dear God, please let her develop a hatred of the manual arts before I have to let that demonic box into my house" tone of voice. I took sewing class four times in summer school and failed every time. I didn't just fail the final project; I failed threading the machine.

Every time, I would say to the instructor, "I am the dumbest person alive and the only thing my sewing machine will ever produce is thread goiters." And every time she would rub my head and say, "There, there. You just haven't had it explained to you correctly." The same portion of the brain that allows some people to think *you don't hate fruitcake, you just haven't had the right one yet* is that portion of the brain that leads sewing instructors to believe the only thing standing between me and sewing proficiency is speaking very slowly. The instructor would open the back of the machine and I, as if staring into an active digestive system, would flinch and avert my eyes.

"Oh," she'd croon, "it's really quite simple. You just put the bobbin up and wind . . . the . . . thread . . . through . . . the . . . hole . . . under . . . the . . . crankshaft . . . halfway . . . to . . . flibst . . . the . . . innermost . . . Jovean . . . moon . . . spin . . . it . . . around . . . this . . . Salvadorean . . . parabola . . . and . . . it . . . comes . . . up . . . here! Now, the bottom one is a little more tricky . . ."

She would do it for me. Then she'd watch me do it eighty or ninety times before realizing someone else in the class had sewn her hand to her shirt or made a bong out of a steam iron, at which point she would leave. I would insert fabric, put my foot on the pedal, and within twenty seconds create a thread-goiter of such density as to render the machine unusable for the rest of the school year. I will become that woman who sends her daughter to sleep-away sewing camp to avoid the look of pity and horror I would earn giving this shiny new sewing machine an intestinal blockage.

Still, I kept trying to be the crafty mom. We made a pinecone Christmas tree. In under a minute I had glued the tree to my hand. I started ineffectually jabbing the pipe cleaner I was supposed to use for tinsel between the tree and my hand, to free it from my skin. It did loosen a bit, but only after I stabbed myself in the palm, leaving a permanent silvery reminder under my life line. It's hard to get excited about homemade ornaments when you're trying to decide if you need an antibiotic booster for Boxing Day.

At one point, Alice was given a book of elegant paper dolls and I, removing them from the page, cut off their heads. This wasn't a complete loss, as it led to a fun afternoon of "Alice dresses the aristocracy during the French Revolution."

A parenting magazine showed a picture of a rock with googly eyes and painted hair attached. In its own way, it was strangely winning. The magazine swore we could do it together. That day, I learned I can attach googly eyes to anything and no matter where I place them, no matter how many times I move them around or align their focus, the effect is that of a mortally wounded soldier on the battlefield, gazing up into your soul, mutely begging you to shoot him.

This all would be easier if Consort were equally incompetent, but he's not. His google-eyed rocks gaze upon mine with scorn. He can cut out paper dolls. He could create a Conestoga mini-wagon that would run on solar power and spark a bidding war between Lilliputian pioneers. In fact, there's a thick file in Alice's brain labeled *THINGS DADDY CAN DO THAT MOMMY CAN'T*. Daddy can drive a stick-shift and Mommy can't. As my mother says, our people don't drive a stick-shift for the same reason that we don't beat our clothing clean against a rock. But the fact remains: Daddy can leap into a stick-shifted car and peel away; Mommy would sit in the driver's seat and wonder why there was an extra pedal on the floor. Daddy can use all those dangerous-looking carpentry tools he has in the garage. He doesn't, mind you, but he could. Pointing out that I have a kitchen full of tools I don't use doesn't make me cooler. Daddy, like some of the more charismatic boys in Alice's class, can make a noise using only his hand and his armpit. Mommy claims she could, but doesn't choose to—which makes no sense because who wouldn't want to make noises with their armpits?

Eventually, we will leave the Craft Age (which comes after the Bronze Age, before the Bronzer Age) and will enter the Higher Math Age, at which point I will lose face all over again. The yawning sense of incompetence and panic that washes over me when confronted with construction paper, pipe cleaners, and glue is as nothing compared to what I will feel when Alice asks for help with her geometry homework. Proofs, theorems, sines, cosines, algorithms—they all blur together in my head, creating a hellish bouillabaisse that will drown the last of my daughter's respect for me. Her father, of course, enjoys higher math thoroughly, so this will be a wonderful bonding time for them. They will make calculus jokes and, after a few seconds, I'll laugh along, nervously and a little too loudly; and because they love me they will take pity on me. One of them will bring out the dusty Conestoga wagon and we'll all look at it as a wheel falls off. Alice will cover my hand with hers and say something kind before she and her father go off to create cold fusion.

Lift. Twist. Pull.

I DON'T KNOW HOW I GOT SO LUCKY, BUT WHEN CONSORT gets sick, he gets sick discreetly. Possessing a high tolerance for discomfort—a trait that might owe something to living with me—he just plugs away until I find myself shouting, "Would you please just get into bed and insert in the IV!" This is, I should note, a loving shout.

A recent illness was different. It was so brutal he went to bed with only modest badgering on my part. He had aches, a dry hacking cough, chills but no fever, and intermittent dizziness. It was as if his immune system was sampling random pages from the *Physician's Desk Reference*. Poor Consort, he was genuinely miserable.

The first night he was sick, we decided Consort would sleep in Alice's room and she would bunk with me. This worked for exactly one night because Alice—though as winning as a stadium filled with Miss Congenialities—has more pointy corners than a starfish. I kept waking up as each of her fifteen elbows found their way into my ribs, spine, and eyes. Add to this her maternally inherited habit of grinding her teeth so forcefully it sounds like a garbage disposal with a spoon stuck in it, and I knew we needed another plan. If Consort was even slightly improved, we'd put her back in her room and I'd take my chances.

The next day, Consort sounded worse and looked almost as bad. His complexion had taken on the shiny, greenish-gray tone of an oyster. We contacted the doctor and he prescribed antibiotics for him. Consort would be contagious for at least another day and probably coughing all night. The sleep issue raised its head again. Consort could have our bed back, Alice would take her pointiness and her grinding back to her own dominion, and I would sleep on the couch. I didn't mind. Our couch has marvelous soporific properties, which you wouldn't think of by looking at it. It's from the 1950s, huge and sinuously curved. When we first got it, I had it upholstered in a fuzzy, bright green fabric, which looked wonderful as a three-by-two-foot sample. Spread across the couch's statement-making size, however, it became a background character from a *Sesame Street* arena show. Or a gigantic, gay amoeba. This was just one in a long list of design mistakes I've made over the years, but when you sit on it you can hear the soft fabric crooning, "Just put your head down. Just for a second. No one will know . . ." Two hours later you wake up with a fuzzy-fabric pattern etched on your face.

This night, I settled Alice into bed and arrayed her stuffed animals around her feet in parade formation. Then I settled Consort in, placing his meds in a similar deployment. I grabbed my favorite pillow and a blanket from the linen closet and headed to the living room. I lit a fire in the fireplace and brewed some herb tea. The room looked welcoming and cozy in a nearly professional way. Even the immense homosexual paramecium looked less weird than usual. Had I placed a sweet grandma on the couch, I could have shot an ad for long-distance telephone service. A blonde model would have sold you Midol.

I crafted a little nest with the blanket and pillow and tucked myself in. Lulabelle loped into the room, came to an abrupt stop, and stared. I don't know what she had been planning but clearly my being there spoiled it. I patted the blanket. She considered her options and sprung up. I scratched her head as I read. Somewhere in the house, Consort coughed in his sleep and Alice stuck her pointy corners into dreamed adversaries. From the outside it probably didn't look like nirvana but it was as close to peace as my family got. That should have been my first clue.

One moment I was scratching between Lu's ears, the next I was removing her nails and teeth from deep in my hand. Lulabelle was gazing directly at me but seeing nothing. Her eyes were solid black marbles. She sank her nails into my hand again and gurgled in delight. This wretched little beast was obviously possessed. I was harboring a psycho cat-zombie, desperate for the life-regenerating properties of human flesh. What could possibly be making our calm, friendly cat so damned weird?

And then I remembered. Catnip!

A month earlier, I'd been invited to a school fund-raiser for a friend's kid. Try as I might, I cannot think of a way to attend these things without spending money on unnecessary stuff. Typically I avoid them like Consort's illness, but if I blew off my friend's fund-raiser I could never guilt her into coming to ours. That's how it works. So there I was, standing in a bustling auditorium trying to decide which I needed less: a free-trade baby rattle or hemp oven mitts. Then I noticed a small collection of cat toys in a basket. Tuning out the poncho-clad mom explaining how these were made by indigenous Peruvian villagers—people who must have been slightly baffled by the concept of "making toys for food to play with"—I grabbed the smallest object on the table.

"And this . . . ?" I asked, holding up a small plastic bag

of something I could only hope was legal in the state of California.

"Organic catnip," she said, pleased I had noticed. "Grown by a prison outreach program. They also raise beets and make fruitcake."

I was unclear of the connection unless it was Things Most People Don't Eat, but I didn't care. For less than ten dollars, I could catch my friend's eye as I slid out the door, waving the unbleached-paper bag indicating I had bought something, and feel no guilt over ambushing her with a fundraising Tupperware catalog later in the year.

When I got home that night, Lulabelle was sleeping on our bed, a black dot of contentment. She wanted nothing more in this world than to continue in a state of perfect bliss. So, naturally, I woke her. I shook out one of the rather suspicious-looking buds and put it in front of her without any expectation of enthusiasm on her part. I had tempted her with catnip toys before, but Lulabelle's attitude had always been, "Wake me when it's thrashing and screaming in fear." The woman who sold it to me swore that its freshness, its lack of pesticides, and its general good karma from having been grown by the formerly oppressed gave it extra moxie.

Lulabelle flicked an ear, extended one paw, and patted the flower around. She stood up and batted it around a little more vigorously. Then she jumped straight into the air, pounced on the bud, flung it skyward, leapt after it, and turning in space, flopped on top of it like a drunken acrobat. I was delighted. For once, I had given a gift where the recipient didn't ask for the receipt. In fact, she was getting a little too pleased with her present. Somewhere between the frantic biting of the bud—followed immediately by attacking my knees—and a series of frenetic wind sprints accompanied by weird guttural shrieks, I decided Lulabelle had enough personality as it was. She didn't need a psychotropic jump-start.

I hid the bag in the office. I was washing dishes an hour later when the cat flew into the kitchen, leapt at my shoulder howling in pure delight, then ran off toward the bedrooms. Something told me she might be driving under the influence again. I checked the office. Lulabelle had pushed open the door, located the bag on its high shelf, torn it open with her claws and teeth, and eaten a few more buds. Summoning my inner drug trafficker, I packaged the bag inside another bag and placed it first in a hanging basket over the kitchen sink and then inside a high cupboard. Both times, within an hour, another bud had been scored and I had a nine-pound, cranked-up Hell's Angel terrorizing my home.

I scanned the house trying to think of a single drawer or cabinet that even the most determined addict couldn't tease open. The linen closet! The doors of the linen closet have been painted so many times over the past eighty years that the accumulated paint has added another quarter-inch or so to each panel. Once they are closed, it takes a very specific *Lift, Twist, Pull* maneuver to open them without injury—a move that had taken me six months to perfect. If Lulabelle figured this out, my concern would not be how to keep her away from the catnip but how we were going to afford college for both the kid *and* the cat. I toyed with the idea of just throwing the bag of murderous fun in the trash, but rejected that on two grounds: one, I don't throw perfectly good *anything* away and two, the vague sense of guilt that I'd be taking away the only pure joy the cat has in which we can all participate. I'm sure she felt equally, exquisitely alive when snapping a bird's neck or screaming at the neighbor's pugs, but I don't see the rest of the family participating in either activity.

So I crammed the bag into the linen closet and promptly forgot about it. The catnip, indifferent to my wish that it would just go away, continued to emit its mysterious vapors deeply into the blankets into which it had been tucked. Now, one of these blankets was covering my body, on top of which was the cat, flopping around like a freshly caught swordfish and living in a paradise only she could see. Every time I went to touch her, to remove her from the head shop that was my blanket, she would bite me. I had two options: to lie very still and wait for the catnip to wear off or to lie very still and wait for the feline assassin to grow bored. Usually, I stay pretty still when I'm sleeping; that night I'm sure I gave every appearance of being guest of honor at my own wake.

The next morning, Lulabelle sprung up from the couch, stretching and yawning. She looked pleased with herself, alert and energized. Having spent the same night reminding myself not to move, I was less than refreshed. My eyes were tiny raisins shoved into dough. My facial skin hung on me like a poncho. I decided that no matter what symptoms Consort exhibited during the day, sleeping in my own bed was still better than having a deranged cat use my foot as a speed bag.

But then Consort coughed. He coughed all day, a rasping and stubborn hack that laughed at all the over-the-counter treatments and at least one prescribed medication. The high-octane cough syrup might have prevented him from operating heavy machinery but it didn't prevent him from coughing. By the time we went to bed, I was resigned to the fact I'd be on the couch again if I had any hope of sleeping at all. Returning to the linen closet, I realized that even though I knew stowing the catnip there had been a bad idea, I hadn't moved it, thus guaranteeing a wide selection of drug-infused bedding. I carefully chose the blanket farthest from the bag o' buds for my next night's sleep.

Stupid woman. As far as Lulabelle was concerned, I was a mountain of warm mammal flesh wrapped in a carapace of catnip. Tonight, along with the ninja attacks, she added a high-pitched gargling sound. It was exactly the noise she made when a squirrel had the audacity to be seen frolicking outside the kitchen window, and now, it seemed, I was in the same category. I slept the fitful sleep of prey.

The next morning, the alarm clock went off like a home invasion. I staggered into the bathroom where a ninety-year-old woman startled me from the mirror. The cat purred and leaned against my leg. I hadn't told Consort about the blanket business. He was feeling bad enough. Besides, I suspect he wouldn't have believed me. When Loodles wasn't under the spell of demon nip, she was almost ludicrously affectionate. Consort's response would have been "Lulabelle? The one getting to third base with your ankles? Noooo . . ." My addicted abuser presented a pretty face to the world. Lifetime would make a movie of my torment.

Consort was officially diagnosed with bronchitis, which meant a new course of antibiotics and at least two more days before I could safely share a bed with him. I shivered. The cat smiled.

After our third night on the couch, the cat began stalking me through the house. She was the lioness and I was the gnu with the gammy leg. My sleep-deprived brain was desperate for a night without ambush; my legs were desperate for a night without puncture. Getting my blankets that night, gazing into the shadows of the linen closet at the catnip bag, it came to me in a flash: I might not get a full night's sleep, but it would be leagues better than what I was getting now.

I lay down on the couch and unfolded the blanket. The cat grabbed the blanket with twenty lethal claws and started to bite furiously. From my pocket, I produced the bag of catnip and opened it. Her head snapped up from her biting. She froze. I removed a bud, wafted it in front of her nose a couple of times. Her eyes glazed over in ecstasy. I threw the bud across the room. Lulabelle sprang from the couch, landing on the catnip bud in one pounce. She spent several happy minutes grinding the bud into psychedelic granules. Then she raced a few laps around the house. Having taken this time to slither into the bed I had made, I lay on the couch, unmolested. Just as I was drifting off, nine pounds of hallucinating predator landed on my back with a thud. I took another bud from the bag tucked into my blanket and flung it across the room. Again, she raced off for the kill, leaving my extremities unmauled.

The same ability that had allowed me, when Alice was an infant, to walk into another room, locate the pacifier, replug the child, and go back to bed without waking up now allowed me to play catnip fetch without leaving a REM cycle.

Consort coughed, although less drastically. Alice thrashed and ground her teeth. Lulabelle dreamt she was Joan of Arc driving the Bolsheviks out of Neptune. And I achieved a flawed but ultimately acceptable night's sleep.

By the next night, Consort was very nearly well. I could safely move off the couch and back into my own bed. I folded my psychedelic blanket one last time and noticed the cat sound asleep on her back, her front paws covering her eyes. I wasn't so far away from my youthful and indulgent past that I didn't recognize a brutal hangover when I saw it. Replace the gnawed-clean catnip bud with an empty flask and a neck full of plastic beads and Lu would have looked perfectly at home slumped in a doorway in the French Quarter. I reached between her paws and gently tried to remove the last remaining bud. Without opening her eyes, without even waking up, she bit me. I tiptoed into the other room, recovered the rest of the stash, and placed it gently next to her sleeping form, an offering to a much loved and easily angered god.

Ye Olde Los Angeles

A FRIEND OFFERED HER MAGNIFICENT HOME TO BE IN-cluded in her neighborhood historical society's fund-raising tour. This is the kind of casually glamorous thing that happens to this friend all the time, and she invited me to join her while she checked out the other houses on the tour. Notice I said *her* neighborhood historical society. My neighborhood doesn't have a historical society. The closest we've come to civic beautifica-tion is an 800 number for abandoned shopping carts. Some-times, one of these carts bears the insignia from a supermarket no longer in business, which, I guess, might qualify it as histori-cal. Anyway, my friend told me to get to her place at 2:30 p.m., when her tour-giving shift ended. I arrived a few minutes early and marched across her spacious front yard past a three-piece Dixieland band and tables laden with punch and cookies. Visi-tors in period dress milled and chatted, sipped punch, and nib-bled cookies. I approached the front door where a historically clad docent said cheerily, "Welcome to the Magnolia House, please put on the booties before entering. The next tour begins in four minutes." She pointed to a basket of what appeared to be huge, fuzzy condoms in a festive blue.

"Actually," I whispered to her, feeling somehow like I was trying to cut in line, "I'm a friend of the owner."

Her heavily lashed eyes widened, but ever so slightly. She asked my name and disappeared into the house. As I waited I watched the people around me slip terrycloth galoshes over their shoes to protect the vintage flooring inside. Another historically clad woman came onto the porch, and at that moment I realized I was the only person on the property not wearing a picture hat and an ankle-length skirt. I tried to strike a historically appropriate pose. It was the least I could do to keep in the spirit of things. The first docent reappeared and nodded my way. "Mrs. G— knows you are here and will be right out," she explained, in a buttery tone. "In the meanwhile, I am going to have to start the next tour. You probably know *all* about the house, so please be patient with me." The other guests looked over at me respectfully as someone who was allowed into the house without paying. As I slipped on my Muppet overshoes, I had the brief and mostly alien sensation of being the coolest person in a thirty-foot radius.

The docent took a square of paper from her historically accurate bag, unfolded it, and began reading. Magnolia House, she announced, was large. Magnolia House had been made using a kind of wood that you hardly see on the West Coast anymore (which, of course, might be related to having been all chopped down to make big houses like Magnolia House). You may have noticed that Magnolia House's front yard has the largest tree in the neighborhood, which, it was said, had been used by the local Native American tribes as a meeting place. We all turned and looked at the tree. The docent then mentioned that a guest on an earlier tour told her it wasn't a native tree so it couldn't have been a Native American meeting place. We all stared at the tree for a second longer, admiring its no-longer-a-meeting-place-but-still-very-attractive qualities. Then we turned back toward Magnolia House. The docent noted that Magnolia

House had been exquisitely restored by the owner. At this point, the docent smiled at me. Apparently, my friend's unflagging ability to find authentic leaded-glass inserts somehow left a residual glow upon me. I tried to look modest but worthy.

Now it was time to go inside. Everyone tightened their fuzzy shoe-condoms and the front door opened. My friend—having spent the required time giving the tour and keeping people from touching her toothpaste—came flying through it. She had transferred her tour obligations to another docent so we could now walk around the neighborhood and check out the other houses.

Half a block later, we approached the next house on the tour and were given the brief external prelude, which involved John Barrymore having owned the house until he lost it in a divorce. Nearly every house on the tour had a history with one of the better divorce lawyers in Ye Olde Los Angeles. English country houses have the Reformation; Los Angeles houses have the Deposition. We walked inside and while everyone else said, "Oooh," I very softly said, "Oh," and instinctively wrapped my arms around my torso. It hadn't occurred to me until just that moment that all of these houses would be filled with such very nice things. I don't do well with very nice things. I am not a bull in a china shop; I am a bull terrier in a china shop, capable of doing far more damage with my small, lively frame than one might think. Hearing the docent tell us about the one-of-a-kind bibelots sitting on the mockingly fragile side table, the mate of which was in the Royal Museum of Flimsy Things in Stuttgart, didn't help. While trying to make myself smaller, I hit the eighteenth-century Irish breakfront with my elbow. The original glass shivered slightly, the inlay appeared to loosen a touch. Because

I didn't want to turn this lovely afternoon into another public lesson about why Quinn can't have nice things, I slithered away from the group and parked myself in a corner behind a solid-looking couch. I stood very straight. I kept my arms at my sides. I tried not to move my head. My historically appropriate character would have been Bridget, the frightened immigrant maid.

This secure perch provided me the unexpected benefit of observing several different tours. The house, it seems, had been in dreadful shape. The present owner had spent much time and, it was understood, wheelbarrows full of thousand-dollar bills to bring the home back to its prime. No continent save Antarctica had been unmolested in pursuit of exactly the right details, which were endless. The tone the docents took was the same tone documentary filmmakers take when covering the Civil War: *be of good cheer during the battles, for we all know how this turns out.* Also, as with certain Civil War buffs, their passions weren't always my passions. When the fifth tour was encouraged to note the original push-button light switches and marvel at how these were only the third push-button light switches to be installed in the city of Los Angeles, my mind started to meander.

I am a terrible shopper for anything of consequence. I'm instinctively drawn toward objects that excite a sense of pity in more reasonable consumers. If the thing to be bought is clean and attractive, my first thought is *Everyone is going to want that* and I steer my quest toward something odd and unsettling, preferably leaking a sticky fluid or bulging ominously at the seams. The dark side of being "of help" is that once you take on the big projects, the big projects sense your soft-heartedness and reward you with some of the most abusive and bizarre behavior ever seen outside the *Prussian Journal of Abnormal Psychology*.

Which explains my house.

I never actually wanted to buy a house. I hate owning things and what is a house but a really big stinking thing with countless smaller things piled inside? All through my twenties, I enjoyed the obligation-free lifestyle of renting, especially the part where when something goes wrong your greatest concern is locating Ivan the maintenance guy before Ivan locates his daily Big Gulp laced with Sterno. The way I understood it, when something went wrong with a house you actually *owned* you were not encouraged to run into the front yard, find the nearest publicly inebriated geezer, and insist it was *his* job to snake your drains.

Both my mother and my accountant grew adamant that handing vast amounts of my meager income to the government was a mortal sin. Not to mention the whole rent versus equity-building argument—a baroque opera my accountant could sing in all its parts. And did. Every quarter. Finally, I was told in no uncertain terms to buy a house. I tried avoiding the inevitable by hating every single house I saw, which wasn't hard. The only good thing I could say about house shopping was that it made dating less depressing.

There were a few options open to me at the time, nearly all of which were unbearable: I could buy a condominium of such anonymity that had I walked into the wrong unit I could have lived there for a week before asking myself, "When did I buy pickled beets?" Or I could buy a real, honest-to-God house with a yard and everything, but it would have been so far away from the actual city that I would visit it only on weekends, spending the remaining five nights a week in my Swedish pied-à-terre parked behind a diner on Sunset. Or, finally, I could buy a house in need of repair in a neighborhood known for a lively mixture of the artsy and the gangtsy. As long as I wasn't absolutely tied to the idea of viable plumbing or a neighbor without a meth lab, I too could pursue the American dream within the city's borders.

The house had been described by the real estate agent as "charming," which I came to understand meant, "You want glass in those windows? Well, la dee dah. Ain't you the Queen of France!" The present owners had self-funded an independent feature that would never find a projector much less a paying audience so they were desperate to sell the house. I walked into the living room, flinched at the stained carpet, winced at the painted-over beams, cowered under the popcorn ceiling, and covered my eyes from the glare of the Home Depot track lighting. The whole effect was that of a back-alley dentist. Yet once we opened the shades (and set them aside as they fell off their hinges), the light streaming in was copious and beautiful.

When the bathroom was last renovated, back in the seventies, the owners must have gotten a killer deal on black tile, black fixtures, and black "wet-look" paint. Frustrated when they couldn't paint the original pink floor tiles, they tried bleaching them instead. This created the appearance of a grimy Big Stick perpetually melting on the bathroom floor. There was a shabbily made soffit suspended over the bathroom sink with a fluorescent fixture humming from within. The soffit was large, curved, and painted high-gloss black. It was as if Death were looming over your shoulder, monitoring your hair loss.

The kitchen "suite" was made up of a couple of small, separate rooms, including the original kitchen and an adjacent space that was once an outdoor porch. The other rooms had a mysterious, aggressively vacant quality. There was a room that the Realtor, an undiagnosed psychotic with a puckish sense of humor, referred to as the "third bedroom." It was an exact duplicate of the room on Ellis Island where they held people with weeping eye infections. There was also a curious little four by six enclosure with five electrical outlets and a built-in, fold-up ironing board longer than the room itself. Electrical outlets were a kind of leitmotif in the house. There was no room without at least five. One small room had ten. They served as a nice counterpoint to the four phone lines into the house, all of which spawned outlets in each room. I assumed this allowed a previous occupant to call four friends at once and brag about how many outlets he had.

The whole house was a big, throbbing "NO," with a heaping helping of "Why is there a working toilet in the bedroom closet?" thrown in for emphasis. And yet, there was that afternoon light in the living room, warm and pervasive without being insistent. Unconsciously, I noted where the Christmas tree would go. At first nearly inaudible, then louder, then drowning out the real estate agent's blather about lot size was a voice in my head saying, *We can fix this.*

I know this voice. It's the same voice that encouraged me to adopt a cat who despised me and was later diagnosed with something called "feline rage." It's the same voice that caused me to take a job with a woman whom I had been warned was as crazy as a shit-house rat, with the added caveat that if I valued my mental health, I'd grab my purse, race to my car, and change my phone number. It's the same voice that picked everyone I dated from seventeen to twenty-seven. This voice sings in a three-part harmony of generosity ("I *should* fix this"), hubris ("I *will* fix this"), and teeth-gnashing naïveté ("I *can* fix this"). It tells me everyone else has failed at fixing something so now it's *my* job. I will spend time and money finding the cat the perfect scratching post even though she showed a preference for my corneas; I shall offer up my self-esteem as brittle Parmesan against the human cheese grater for whom I work; I shall live on Twizzlers and Diet Cokes while my boyfriend writes his romantic comedy about mutant robots; I will walk into home ownership with my eyes wide open, knowing I will spend vast sums of time and money trying to elevate this home from "charming" to habitable.

Back on the historical tour, the docents had a seemingly endless array of happy-accident anecdotes:

> *The owners thought the original Tiffany sconces had been sold, but they happened to find them in a box in the servants' quarters behind the shoe closet.*

> *The chandelier the owner impulsively purchased at a Vatican tag sale twenty years ago perfectly matched the window treatment in the formal foyer.*

> *They removed the paneling in the library to have it re-carved by celibate Neapolitan woodworkers and found a vault stuffed with money and the deed to another, even more historic, home in Paris.*

My renovation surprises were less serendipitous:

Do you know you have a cat skeleton under there?

The plumber was standing in the back doorway, the dust and cobwebs from the crawl space forming a kind of gray mantilla. I internally replayed what he said several times, trying to find some way I could have misunderstood it. I played it safe and went with repeating the noun and not the other noun.

"Cat?"

He mulled my question while totaling up the bill. "Maybe a skunk, but probably a cat. It's just bones," he said hastily, mistaking my look of general horror with a fear of putrefaction. "I'm just telling you so you can tell the electrician."

"Why will I be telling the electrician?" I asked with perfect enunciation.

The plumber frowned. "Because," he said slowly, "he might want to know before he puts his hand on it?"

"I'm sorry, that was unclear," I said, terribly calmly. "Why will I be calling the electrician?"

"Because," he said cheerfully, as he continued adding up my now very long bill, "next to the dead cat, there's some wire down there which is kind of smoldering. I'd get someone in today."

A week later, I was sitting in the kitchen glaring at the breakfast-nook shelves. The smoldering electrical wire had turned out to be a harbinger of massive and systemic electrical failure, possibly due to the multiple extra outlets illegally installed in each room. The cost to fix this was gruesome and had the added aggravation of improving the overall appearance of the house not one whit. After all the old wires were removed and new, nonsmoldering ones installed in their place, my house would look exactly the same, minus the burning-wire smell, which hadn't bothered *me* at all. The worst thing that might have happened was that the house would have burnt down, which was starting to sound like a good idea. All I could think was: *Please God, just let me improve one single thing in this stupid house that someone can actually see.*

Which led to the breakfast nook. A previous owner had decided to make his own shelves. These shelves were constructed of some sort of toothpick/Kleenex aggregate, which caused them to sag limply against the wall like a faded Tennessee Williams heroine. After maybe three weeks in the house, I had grown so tired of watching my shelves suffer the vapors I decided something had to be done. I grabbed Consort, who was still trying to figure out why the garage door opened when we used the toaster.

"I hate the shelves in the breakfast nook," I grumbled, preparing to launch into how the shelves were the physical embodiment of everything evil.

"Then get rid of them," he said matter-of-factly, shaking the toaster.

I gasped. "I can do that?"

"Why not? They're ugly. They aren't original. You hate them. And it's *your* house."

I stood a little straighter. It was my house. I was part of the fastest-growing demographic in the United States—single women who were home owners—and I, as a single-woman home owner, was going to make a home-improvement decision!

"I am going to remove those stupid shelves," I announced. I then said, "I have no idea how to remove those stupid shelves."

Consort introduced me to the crowbar before going back to his own house, where nothing was dead and wall sockets didn't spontaneously combust. Crowbarring looked simple enough. I was to put the wedge-y end of the crowbar between the crappy shelf and the wall, and gently pry them apart. The crappy shelf would fall to the ground and I would dance with glee and female empowerment. I put the wedge-y bit in and pulled. The wood groaned slightly, but the shelf remained in place. I pulled a little harder and felt something like movement. I yanked, and the shelf came off the wall. Unfortunately, the wall also came off the wall. I fell back against the kitchen table and stared in dismay into a gaping hole. I was looking at outside plaster, which confused me. Wasn't there supposed to be some sort of wood between the inside wall and the outside wall? And speaking of wood, shouldn't there be some sort of lumber holding up this corner of the room?

"There are termites, which eat from the top down. Another kind eats from the bottom up. This house has both. About thirty years' worth, from the looks of it." Thus spoke the Exterminator, who had been recommended by the Lawyer who had been put on retainer to talk to the previous Exterminators with an eye toward determining whether the previous Exterminators who had declared the house termite-free had been criminally incompetent or merely criminal. The Lawyer's Exterminator eventually led to the Contractor. I now had many new friends, nearly all of whom charged by the hour. The Contractor was impressed by how long the house had managed to sustain itself without any actual wood holding up that corner. By the time he'd pulled away enough plaster to find lath in the wall, he had created a hippopotamus-sized hole in my kitchen wall.

While waiting for the Exterminator to exterminate and the Contractor to contract, Consort put a plastic tarp over the hole. The outer wall had more than a few cracks so when the wind blew the tarp would expand and contract like a giant blue lung. This just added to the sense that the house was alive and anxious for revenge against all the humans who had abused it for seventy years. I plugged a microwave into one of the seven outlets in my bedroom and hid there as much as possible. One night, on a trip to the fridge, I stood by the tarp and could hear termites copulating.

When I was young, the idea of marriage scared the hell out of me. I just knew that I would be walking back down the aisle, the celebration march playing, my loving groom on my arm, and I'd catch the eye of the date of one of my wedding guests and I'd think, *No, wait!* You *are the man of my dreams, not this well-meaning simp with whom I agreed on a silverware pattern. I've made a terrible mistake and it's going to cost all my dignity and a bucket of money to make this problem go away.* So I chose never to get married, opting when the time came for a state I like to call "Living in sin with basic cable." But, like some mythological tale about the futility of skirting one's destiny, I escaped my fate as a trapped wife only to find myself married to an incontinent ninety-year-old with open sores and anger-management issues. My house.

"I thought I was ready for this," I told the house. "But I was wrong. It's not you, it's me. You're great, but I want to see other houses," I said tentatively.

The house, indifferent to my suffering, continued to decay and take me with it.

Every attempt to improve the house opened a new faucet of pain. When I bought the place, the kitchen drawers featured aggressively ugly handles. They had kind of a *You find me unattractive? Well, joke's on you, chump because there are seventeen more of me on this wall alone* thing going on. The kitchen had only two shelves of usable storage but enough drawers to serve as a morgue for every Barbie in California. In a fit of post-termite despair, I removed about half the handles only to discover that their width matched no other handle in any known hardware marketplace on earth. When I tried to drill new holes to fit actual handles manufactured here in the three-dimensional universe, I discovered the drawers' faceplates were made of some kind of pressed talcum powder, which exploded on contact with a drill bit. Of course, I couldn't put the old handles back because I had thrown them away. I couldn't put on new handles until I removed all the weird faceplates and it didn't make sense to do that until I renovated the kitchen, which I couldn't do because I needed the money I had set aside for kitchen renovation to patch the hippo-sized hole in the unrenovated kitchen without drawer handles, whose owner was pouring herself a rather tall drink.

Back on the historic tour, each house was a beautiful testament to its current owner's care and, we all understood, mountains of cash. Whether he was home or not, each house stood as the living embodiment of its owner's fine design eye, his acute aesthetic sense, and his ability to bill six hundred dollars an hour, thirty-six hours a day. I stood in this magnificent residence and watched the light play across the Persian carpet and bounce off the French silk upholstery. Had this house been a person, she would have been chic, self-confident, and intimidatingly poised, alluding to her recent trip to Lake Como with casually dropped quotes from Blake and Thoreau. My house was a dilapidated soul living behind a bus stop, dressed in a hostess skirt fashioned of plastic grocery bags, railing against the Warren Commission.

Ultimately, that was what I hated most about my house. It was disorganized. It wasn't conventionally appealing. It was inclined to hold grudges and then punish the wrong people. No wonder the idea of marriage always gave me the yips. One way or another, I knew I'd end up marrying myself.

Somehow, realizing how horrible everything had become turned the tide. It went from being "the horrible house" to "my horrible house," to, finally, "my house." I began to notice the afternoon light again and discreetly avoided the laundry room. We reached a rapprochement, the house and I. It doesn't mention my puffy morning eyelids, and I don't bring up its lack of closet space. This might not be a marriage based on deep passion or unconditional love, but I was starting to laugh at its jokes.

Having finished the tour, we stepped outside as a group and removed our shoe condoms, leaving them flattened and spent in the basket awaiting the next troop of period-dressed Peeping Toms. I squinted against the bright sunlight and burrowed in my purse for sunglasses. Something behind the hedge caught my eye. A shadow or—I leaned in for a closer look—perhaps a crack? Perhaps a break in the foundation that would lead to the entire front half of the house falling off as neatly as a slice of aged cheddar? Or maybe it was a nest of homicidal yellow jackets, seconds away from bursting open, sending thousands of enraged insects swarming into the house through the hand-carved French doors and setting up shop in the original dumbwaiter? *Please, oh please, let it be black mold.*

I leaned in over the heirloom roses (original to the house, from a cutting of a bush reputedly pruned by Anne Boleyn) and peered more closely at the dark spot. No, it was just a shadow. A shadow from the original, solid copper, custom-milled downspout. All was still flawless.

But, wait. What was that movement under the delicately carved marble foot plate? I leaned in farther and rejoiced at what I saw. Slipping my sunglasses high on my nose, I congratulated myself that at least *I* didn't have cockroaches. Thus encouraged, I headed home.

In Less Than Glowing Terms

WE CELEBRATE ALICE'S HALF-BIRTHDAY IN THE SAME RES-
taurant every year. We have an attachment to this place because
Consort and I had taken Alice there on her six-month birthday.
Until that night, she had been a placid and mostly silent accessory
in a molded car seat. That very evening, in that very restaurant,
she unveiled her shriek for the first time. It sounded like a stadium full of enraged dolphins with the amplifiers cranked up to
full volume. For the next year, we didn't dine in any restaurant
as a family. Every year since, we return to that same place to
celebrate whatever developmental stage she's in, and that she
doesn't make that noise anymore.

On this most recent half-birthday, I met Consort and Alice
at the restaurant. Consort and I treat parenting as a relay race,
with Alice as the baton. Alice and I go to Place A where I leave
her for a music lesson, then I go to Place B, with Consort arriving at Place A fifty-five minutes later to pick her up. We then
meet at Place C where he hands Alice to me and I hand him his
dry cleaning. Then she and I go to Place D, and he goes wherever he goes when I'm not making him meet us places. That
day, he'd picked her up at her friend's house on the way home
from work. This meant that for once I had a chance to actually
make an attempt to improve my appearance. You wouldn't believe how much extra personal time you can find if you aren't

detangling little-girl hair and vetoing outfits that include shorts and party shoes.

I rolled up to the restaurant just as they were arriving. Alice raced to fling herself upon me but came up short about a foot away. She leaned back, squinted at me, frowned, and pointed an accusing finger at my face. "There's something wrong with your eyes," she said worriedly. "They're all dark and shadowy."

"That's eyeliner, sweetie," I said briskly. "If Mommy were better organized, you'd see it more often."

Consort said loyally, "I think Mom looks very pretty."

But my kid wasn't up to blindly toeing the party line. She persisted, "Why would you want to make your eyes look so tiny and tired? It's just weird."

I said, "Because I was under the impression that it improved my appearance. Thank heavens you were here to clarify that I was completely mistaken."

"You should ask Araminta's mother where she gets her makeup. She's really pretty."

I had heard about Araminta's mother. As always, I restrained myself from noting that I, too, might be really pretty if my ass fat were injected into my face three times a year.

I have never been conventionally attractive. I know this for several reasons. First, I know this because my vision is nearly perfect and mirrors exist. I also know this because I live in Los Angeles, where the prettiest people from every town in the world converge to find work as actors. Some of them learn how to act. Others find long and lucrative careers on daytime soaps. The rest teach yoga. Many eventually meet other nearly flawless people and they breed together, creating a new generation of the

super-attractive, quite a few of whom were in school with me.
Had there been no mirrors and no soap offspring, I still would
have known I wasn't traditionally beautiful because the entertainment industry kept telling me so. From the age of fourteen
onward, I was reading for the part of the wacky sidekick. You
know her as Rhoda Morgenstern, Ethel Mertz, or Jane Hatha-
way. We exist to pop our heads through doorways and say
things like, "Not with *my* towel, you don't!" and to help the female lead hide the Russian mail-order bride she inadvertently
ordered online from her fiancé's parents.

After a few years of being professionally unattractive, I
would begin to open scripts with the timidity of someone opening a can of soda that had been rolling around in the trunk. Few
things in life are certain, but I was reasonably sure that my character was going to be described in less than glowing terms:

Dumpy. Plain. Homely. Unsightly. Frizzy. Clumsy.

I don't think any part I was reading for was ever described
as repugnant or scrofulous—which might have pleased me for
no better reason than imagining some writer paging through a
thesaurus—but any other way of saying, "But she has a great
sense of humor," they said.

I actually got one of these parts. My first scene found me,
Wacky Friend, whining to the lead, Pretty Girl, about how I
didn't want to go to the beach with her because she looked so
much better than I did. I even had an emotional little mono-
logue about how I was a tragic flat-chested thing and she was
this vixen, this goddess, this paragon of female comeliness.

There was one big problem: one of us was flat-chested, and it wasn't me. Yes, she was far prettier than I was and the thick glasses they glued to my nose weren't going to help any, but she was a tiny slip of a thing with the build of the ballerina she had been. We did the first rehearsal reading, and I noticed a worried glance shoot between the director and writer. Illogically, I hoped they would cut the whole speech of self-abasement and allow me to merely be unattractive without making me talk about it for half a page. I got the script revisions. My speech was now about how I didn't want to go to the beach with her because she was the perfect weight and I was only five pounds lighter than the Statue of Liberty.

Knowing you exist as the aesthetic Goofus to another person's Gallant does eventually wear upon your self-esteem. Every once in a while, I would find something left of my spine and proclaim, "That's *it*! I'm not reading for another part where the character enters every room scarfing a bag of Oreos and predicts she'll die alone and be eaten by her cats." But after a few months of arctic silence, it would dawn on me; there were no other roles for me. They weren't looking for twenty-year-olds to play the crusading defense attorney, the impatient but secretly kind neurosurgeon, or the police detective with a haunted past. They were looking for the hot girl or the pity date. More maddening, I wasn't even getting the pity date roles. This had something to do with my refusing to have a wardrobe of unflattering pants and Scrunchies to wear to such interviews and partially because—and I mean this with all kindness and generosity—I was reading against some seriously ill-favored individuals. However bad I was going to look after putting on an orange shirt with ruffles, they were already there. I couldn't pity them too much, though, because being professionally plain had bought them very nice houses in the less-fashionable canyons.

For a while, I comforted myself that I fell only slightly outside Hot Girl. In my mind, I lived adjacent to Hot Girl, in Cute Girl. Cute, it seemed to me, was attainable. Cute was a wide and forgiving land, which allowed a girl entry with nothing more than a winning smile, decent cleavage, and brushed hair. I was cute, I comforted myself, and there just wasn't a place for cute. Then one day I read for a pilot where I actually read for the lead. It was different because they would actually have the merely cute read for the lead. This was possible because they had created a variation of the wacky friend: the wacky *hot* friend who makes up for being really hot by being really slutty, and possibly French. Having provided sufficient stroke fuel in the second lead, they could audition actresses of mere cuteness to star. It was all very exciting.

I read acceptably well. They laughed in the right places. I felt I had done all I could do and hoped that my lip gloss brought me within striking distance of "I'd do her." Later that day, I got a call from my agent. She started off by sighing. Instinctively, I grabbed the bottle of wine and a large glass.

"Well," she began, "they loved you."

"They loved you," in Los Angeles means, "You didn't set their couch on fire."

"But," she said, and stopped.

I poured.

"But they need someone attractive for the role."

Because I am the same person who keeps sticking her tongue

on the canker sore, to see if it's still incredibly painful, I sought clarification.

"That's what they said? 'Attractive'? They didn't say, 'More attractive'?"

"No, they said 'attractive.'"

Had they said they were going for "more attractive," I could have consoled myself with the delusion that it was a matter of degrees between me and Hot Girl. But saying they were going with "attractive" only led to the nasty question, "And that makes me . . . ?"

"Anyway," the agent continued, eager to get on to making other calls and destroying other people's hopes. "They just put out an offer to Valerie Bertinelli."

Methodically, I refilled the wineglass to the rim.

"So," I said thoughtfully, "I can safely assume I am less attractive than Valerie Bertinelli."

"Great. We're on the same page," my agent said in relief. "Gotta go. Love you. Mean it. Bye."

Valerie Bertinelli is, on all accounts, a charming woman. Her hair is marvelously thick and bouncy. Her smile is adorable. I believe she has dimples. But until that moment, had you asked, I would have sworn to you that she and I both dwelt in the land of Cute, both equally blessed in that department. Now I was finding out I had set up my camp in the no-man's-land between Cute Girl, Ugly Friend, and Thing that Demands Payment in Order to Walk over Its Bridge.

I drank wine and ate buttercream frosting from a can. An hour later, tipsy and slightly sticky, I called my most patient male friend. He made the mistake of answering.

"What is wrong with me? And don't try to sound like your housekeeper telling me you're out of town, because I know it's you," I said without preamble.

"I don't know," he said. "Is this a riddle?"

"What's wrong with my appearance?"

He thought. I held my breath.

"Nothing's wrong. You're cute."

"Thank you," I said. "Because I just had the most annoying conversation with my agent."

I related the entire story, minus the frosting. He growled sympathetically in all the right places.

"That is such crap," he barked. "You're fine."

"Wait a moment," I said, glancing around the kitchen for any open wine bottle, "am I *cute* or am I *fine*?"

"Cute, fine, whatever," he replied. Like most heterosexual males, he sensed but rarely understood why the emotional room temperature dropped thirty degrees.

"No, not whatever," I yelped. "Cute is acceptable. Fine is not. God, just poison my food, why don't you. My appearance is fine? So, I'm like a sweater from Talbots or a meal from the Olive Garden? I am the physical equivalent of a Ford Taurus? FINE?"

I heard what sounded like someone tapping his forehead against a kitchen table.

"Quinn, we're platonic friends and I haven't had a date in two months. Unless you are suddenly going to show up at my door wearing lingerie and Lakers tickets, I'm not getting any further into this. You're cute. You're fine. Live with it."

"If I'm cute and fine, then why doesn't anyone sober ever make a pass at me at a bar?"

This was, without qualification, true. At some critical moment after a young man's seventh Jägermeister but before he found himself explaining to the nice officer why he was taking a little nap in a grocery cart, he would find me terribly attractive. This led to my being the recipient of some of the most inappropriate overtures ever seen outside a pack of feral dogs. In my bar-hopping years, I had a young man stagger up to me and offer to burp me his phone number. Another, noting my lack of height, thought of several ways he could use that to his advantage, carnally. He then shouted these ideas to his friends, who had already left the bar, so he shouted at them again, more loudly. It seemed I became attractive only long after the last working brain cell had turned out the light.

I heard him pour coffee.

"I'll tell you, but you won't like it."

I waited and ate a little more frosting.

"You . . . wait, I've got to find milk."

He rustled around in his fridge. I heard pouring. He slurped and then spoke. "You have this vibe. Any man in a bar looks at you and thinks, 'She's cute, but she'd only have sex with me so she could eat me afterwards.' "

We all waited to see if that was it.

"Like a praying mantis," he added, for clarification.

"You're making that up. Just to make me feel better."

"Oh, no," he said cheerfully. "It's pretty obvious, if you're a straight man. The reason the drunks hit on you is because by that point in the evening either they don't pick up on the vibe anymore, or they figure being the victim of cannibalism is a small price to pay to get laid. But looks-wise, you're fine."

Over the next week, I quizzed a few male friends. While none of the others specifically said I was the kind of girl to make a post-coital snack of my date, all of them agreed my appearance was well within the normal range but that I might want to do something about this terrifying aura I emitted. Slowly, it occurred to me that the problem might have something to do with my being an actress.

Acting is a bad boyfriend. The kind of boyfriend who trashes your car, knocks up your kid sister, and ruins your credit. Acting takes and takes and takes to the point where any person with the teensiest bit of self-awareness finally says, "To hell with this. I'm moving back to Billings to make a go of strip-mining." Only then, when Acting realizes that you're nearly out the door, does it briefly pull itself together. You get a job, maybe two, and Acting croons in your ear, "Baby, it's going to be different this time." And you think, *Hey, I can make this work, my luck has turned.* So you refund the one-way ticket to Billings, and Acting, knowing that you have given up all power again, promptly seduces your ex-boyfriend.

Acting isn't even nice to the pretty. For a while when I was younger, I worked as an assistant to a commercial casting director. It was a pleasant job; my boss was one of three sane people in all of Los Angeles, and the job required very little of my brain. Mostly, I herded actors from room to room—I was a border collie for the comely. The only tedious days were when the advertising executives would come to town to make their final casting decisions. Between their underlying fears of being fired for not having created a campaign that was simultaneously edgy and mainstream, and their manic urgency to make dinner reservations each night for the hottest restaurant in town, advertising executives were an exhausting lot. Once, we had been casting a campaign for the face of a major makeup line. The models didn't have to talk, move, or even apply the product. They merely had to stand there and be flawless. Over the course of three weeks, we had seen every female in Los Angeles under the age of twenty who made a living from possessing perfectly symmetrical features. In my life, I had never been so certain of my status as a plain girl.

We brought in the final five candidates. One by one, they stood in front of the camera, turned in profile, smiled, then turned the other profile. Our cameraman pushed in so close their skin resembled a soft Saharan landscape, flawlessly flat and monochrome across the entire screen. Each girl was perfect in her own way. Each could have been using her eggs to start a new race of humans. The only question was, which variation of perfect did these ad guys want?

The last model left. Within a minute, it was determined that each man at the table had his favorite and would accept no other girl to be the client's apotheosis. In order to win others to his opinion, he would have the casting director replay the tapes of the other four models, and then he'd start to nitpick.

"Her nostrils aren't exactly even."

"I think her eyelashes could be longer."

"Look at her chin again in profile. It's a little weak."

"You see how her hair draws attention to her puffy earlobes?"

Each suit would defend his choice, or slice away at the others. Two hours later, they regretfully told my boss that none of them would work because none of them was quite perfect enough. Outside of this room, each of these men would have written to Penthouse Forum had any of these young beauties even said "Hello" to him, but in this magical world, they held all the power. These flawless Helens could not only *not* launch a thousand ships, they couldn't make next month's rent without unanimous approval. Eventually, the ad agency hired the one girl who hadn't been available for the callback. Without her physical presence, they had nothing to tear down.

I had forgotten about all this until I was coated in a layer of cheap chardonnay and French V'nilla Crème Frosting. [The missing "A" stands for "Aren't you glad you don't know we get our 'Vanilla' flavoring from the Jet Propulsion Laboratory?"] I wasn't the smartest person in the unemployment line, but I wasn't a masochist, either socially or professionally. If you keep telling me how fat, unattractive, and generally misshapen I am, eventually I'm going to stop returning your calls. Los Angeles was filled with people prepared to sell their beloved grandmother into slavery for a chance to read for a feature. I came to realize that I wasn't one of those people. The obvious problem with my chosen profession was that I wasn't physically perfect. The less obvious problem was that I didn't love acting anymore. I didn't even like it. I had finally noticed that Acting, the bad boyfriend, wasn't all that cute himself.

It took me another ten years after I stopped acting to realize that my friend had been right: I was fine. I was attractive enough. When you're raised in a community where not one person is *anything* enough (rich, thin, young, powerful, beautiful, etc.), it's strange and liberating to discover that no one outside the entertainment industry thinks about nostril symmetry. Most people have a very realistic expectation of how pretty people should be, and how boring a topic it is to dwell on. Civilians may notice what you look like, but pretty soon they start noticing who you are.

For years, I've watched actor friends panic and start to get things tightened and fluffed. What's distressing is the ridiculously early age at which this panic sets in. An eye-lift at thirty-three doesn't make you look twenty-three, it makes you look alarmed. Then again, if you're holding off intimations of the grave at thirty-three, you have every right to be a little nervous. Today, my appearance is my hobby and not my business. Emotionally, this is neutral territory. In the appearance wars, it's good to be Switzerland. So of course, I gave birth to a little girl with her own set of sartorial impulses, someone who had been hoping for Donatella Versace on the other end of the umbilical cord.

Alice, Consort, and I were now in the restaurant. Either the lighting was better or the roll she was gnawing improved her mood because Alice scrutinized me once more. "The eyeliner isn't too bad," she finally announced. "It brings out the green in your eyes."

I thanked her, wondering as I often do about how my and Consort's genetic material produced an elementary-school beauty editor.

"But," she said, patting my hand in a businesslike way, "we have to do something about your hair."

Like a Tattoo on Your Butt

THE APPOINTMENT HAD BEEN FOR ME. I WAS FOURTEEN years old and having one of my stubborn sinus infections. The fact that I was averaging four such infections a year meant that within minutes of the first bacterium wandering near my sinus cavity my mother and I could diagnose the infection with confidence. The doctor, however, stubbornly refused to take our word for it and made me come to his office. He could only get paid for stating the obvious if he and I were in the same room. We had the whole process down to a ritualized call-and-response, which took less than a minute:

DOCTOR: Coughing?

QUINN: Yes.

DOCTOR: Congestion?

QUINN: Yep.

DOCTOR: Fever?

QUINN: Of course.

DOCTOR: Bad breath?

QUINN'S MOTHER: Low tide.

He would then declare I had a sinus infection and my mother and I would feign surprise. This time, while he was writing out the usual prescription—something the pharmaceutical company should have named after me as a token of its gratitude—my mother asked to talk about another matter. I was sent to wait outside. Being fourteen, I waffled between a sense of outrage that they were talking about me behind my back and a hope that someone in the waiting room might think I was eighteen. It never occurred to me that my mother and our doctor might be discussing anything besides me.

Looking back, I remember for the next week or so my mother's fuse was especially short and susceptible to ignition. Generally thick-skinned, she had become abrupt and snappish, but since fourteen is an age not known for its penetrating interest in the motivations of adults, this didn't affect me one bit. It was two weeks after the sinus appointment when she sat me down for "a talk." I had no idea what the topic was going to be but I sensed it wasn't *I finally got you that pony you always wanted*. Her expression was neutral and direct—the expression she saved for rotten things. I racked my brain for whatever I had done wrong and toyed with preemptive sobbing.

"When we went to the doctor last time," she began, fixing her eyes on me, "I had him check out my throat, because my glands had been swollen for a while. He sent me to another doctor, who did a biopsy." My heart flopped against my rib cage. She continued, "It turns out that I have lymphoma."

My mother kept talking while I drifted in and out. Rarely in my life had I felt more acutely alive. I swear I could feel my hair growing. I could see her lips move and hear every single world she spoke, I just couldn't make the words add up to anything. I heard "chemotherapy" and felt her fingers tap my wrist to draw my attention; I had been staring off into space. This brought me back to, "We're not going to tell anyone I have cancer. Everyone will treat me like I'm going to die and I'm not going to die. So it's better that no one knows." I nodded. I could not see how people wouldn't know, but maybe she was giving me good news. Maybe this particular cancer was so inconsequential that you could have it and keep it to yourself and a few specially chosen loved ones. Maybe this lymphoma thing was like a tattoo on your butt.

Then she said, "I'm not going to die and leave you alone" and I thought, *Crap, I would be alone, wouldn't I?* Papa had died five years earlier and both my parents were only children. But that didn't matter, because lymphoma wasn't that big a deal and we weren't going to tell anyone and she wasn't going to die. She repeated what I hadn't absorbed the first time around. She needed six months of chemotherapy. She would do it on the way to the office in the morning. It would be no big deal. It would begin the next day.

My mother went to hug me, but I shook my head. I was too aware of my own skin and heart and life right now. I really couldn't stand the thought of feeling another living thing. Human contact would have been overwhelming.

Years before, when she had applied for her current job, "Must have my own bathroom" certainly wasn't on my mother's wish list; but, as luck would have it, the only office available when she started happened to have its own private bathroom. This wasn't the executive bathroom. It wasn't even a nice bathroom—the sink was a mural of rust stains and using the toilet required balancing oneself on a stack of toner cartridges—but by the second day of chemotherapy my mother was very grateful for its proximity.

Never a large person, my mother lost nearly twenty pounds

in three weeks. By the second week, her hair was starting to fall out. By the fourth week, she was almost hairless. Within a month, I had a fragile, vomiting, bald mother. The hair loss extended to her eyebrows and eyelashes, giving her the effect of having been partially erased. During this entire time not one single coworker asked after her health. I like to think this was owing to discretion on their part, but it's more likely because fourteen-year-olds aren't the only humans incapable of seeing anyone but themselves.

When her hair started to go, my mother and I spent a Saturday visiting every single wig store in Los Angeles County. There seemed to be three colors of wig: a light-absorbing black, a coppery red Lucille Ball would have rejected as too garish, and beige. Regardless of color, every wig tended to be cut into a shape resembling an old lady's swim cap and had the effect of informing everyone in a visible radius that you were wearing artificial hair. After the last store on our roster, we got back into the car and I looked over at my mother. In her youth, she had been a runway model and even after she stepped off her last catwalk, she continued to possess the style and grace of someone who expected to move through life looking good. Now, nothing fit her stressed frame; no color flattered her ashen skin. She was living in someone else's body, wearing someone else's clothes. Her expression staring out over the steering wheel was one I had never seen before on her in my life. She looked beaten. The temperature in the parked car was, conservatively, six hundred degrees. The combination of this sudden sauna-like heat and her exhaustion from the chemotherapy and futile wig-shopping caused my mother to look nearly dead. Frightened, I tried to lift her spirits.

"That last one wasn't as bad as some of the others," I piped, but my voice died away as I watched her face crumple, her head lean against the steering wheel. She sobbed in terror while I sat there, sweating, breathing hard, and shredding the list of American Cancer Society–approved wig shops between my trembling fingers.

A few days later, I began having weekly conversations with my half-brother—the grown son of my father's first marriage. He was a good guy, kindhearted and funny, but I could count on two hands the number of times we'd been in each other's company. My mother wasn't having me call him in Boston so I could reconnect with my snow-shoveling, Celtics-following, letter-R-dropping roots. Without ever being told so specifically, I understood he'd take me in if she didn't survive. That didn't seem so ludicrous anymore. We would make small talk and I would think about what it would be like to live in Boston, to ask my brother where my mittens were, to have to say to people, "He's my brother. I don't have any other family."

I kept my promise to my mother. I told no one she was sick. One night, a nurse came to the house to take an extensive medical history for a university study. It seemed my mother's lymphoma was quite rare. Hours later, the nurse told my mother, "I'll hand this in but I have to tell you, there's no good reason why you got sick." The nurse may have been mystified, but the sheer statistical oddness of my mother's condition confirmed what had already been running through my head. My father, a healthy man, had dropped dead of a heart attack at a relatively young age. My mother had developed a rare cancer seemingly out of the blue. Random bad things were going to happen to the people I loved and needed. I decided not to care about anyone new.

During all this time, of course, I was in high school. I attended an especially well-regarded private school, one of those places that get fifty worthy applicants for every available spot. I still have no idea why I was there. I am not being modest; my academic record up to this point had been a paean to the life of the underachiever, and my mother was in no position to endow a small opera house should they accept me. The harsh reality was that I didn't even want to be there. I wanted to be acting. But my mother had this charmingly retro idea that she was raising a person, not an actress. I was told I would be going to school like other people my age. So there I was, observing my classmates with the emotional remove of a cultural anthropologist.

In my mind, my peers were an exasperating mixture of worldly and naïve. Owing to their parents' choices, my schoolmates had a deep understanding of California divorce and custodial laws, the exact make and model of the German sports car they were expecting on their sixteenth birthdays, and the most creative off-label uses for certain prescription drugs. But when it came to actual world events—which is to say anything that didn't specifically improve their chances of breaking into the Ivy League—they were as sheltered as nuns. Their job was to do well in school and get accepted into the kind of college that would make their extremely successful parents forget they had taken seven years to graduate from State.

One particular classmate—I'll call her Debra—produced in me the sensation of chewing on tinfoil while listening to an extended club mix of nails on a chalkboard. And that was in my best of moods. Debra came with a list of disagreeable personality traits, and topping the list was the fact that she was the least intellectually curious person I had ever met. Of course, this also meant she had a near-perfect aptitude for excelling at high school. The teachers would speak and her brain would tranquilly and unquestioningly record every single fact, flagging each data point to spit back verbatim at such future time of the teachers' choosing. When asked her opinions on a more general topic, Debra would reprise the teacher's most recent lecture, right down to the "Ums" and the "I means," to which the teacher would beam back in pure pedagogical joy. Her mastery of the high school academic game only confirmed my suspicions that a properly socialized African gray parrot could make it to Brown.

One day during my mother's third month of chemo, when her hair was completely gone and her skin was the color of a saltine, I was sitting in the cafeteria eating lunch when Debra came flying through the door, sobbing uncontrollably. A few classmates, alert to the pleasures of drama by proxy, ran to her side. Debra remained frozen in the doorway, wailing. Finally, she managed to force out a few words.

"I . . . got . . . an . . . eighty- . . . *nine*!"

The sobs began anew. It took a few minutes, but everyone in a three-mile radius of the cafeteria finally got the full story. Our class had taken an English test. For the first time in Debra's life, she had scored less than a ninety. While the rest of us were eating lunch, she had been begging the teacher for the extra point to protect her sterling average. She had even offered to do another report for extra credit—she just wanted *one* point—but the teacher was resolute. Debra's academic record now included a B-plus, and it was going to stay that way until her dying day.

Freshly outraged, she blubbered, "Why do the worst things

always happen to me? I am so unlucky. This is the worst thing
that could ever happen to anyone."

I finished chewing my apple. Debra's thick, waist-length
hair flipped from side to side as she bemoaned her awful fate.
Even through her tears, her face was round and smooth and vibrant with health. I felt a sudden pressing need not to hear her
voice anymore. I got up to leave and was forced to sidle around
her and her support coven still clustered near the doorway. Seeing a new person next to her, and assuming I was there to provide more comfort, she turned to me and moaned, "Oh, Quinn,
you don't know how easy you have it."

"Quinn, why did you choke Debra?"

The vice principal had a year-long relationship with me, and
it was nearly all bad. She liked the sensitive kids. If you were a
girl who wrote bad poetry or cut yourself, or a boy who felt your
best in grandmother's long-line girdle, she couldn't find enough
ways to love you. She'd eat lunch in her office with you. She'd
hold your cigarettes during school hours. She'd help stage your
intervention. She just adored the big loud messes who then
pulled it together and got into a reputable second-tier college
and became active, generous alumni. She didn't like students
who were also actors. She told me the first time we met that she
had voted against my attending the school. Oddly enough, the
fact that *I* had also voted against my attending her school didn't
bond us, nor did my observing out loud that she liked actors
well enough when these actors were parents and they were writing big checks for the scholarship fund. By the time I answered
her question, "What is your problem with authority figures?"

by saying "I have no problem with authority figures when I have some respect for the person wielding the authority," she was counting the minutes until I screwed up big time. Having a star student come streaking into her office claiming I tried to kill her, with five eyewitnesses corroborating that they thought they saw *something* . . . This was a gift from heaven. She leaned back in her chair and squinted at me.

After a long moment, I replied sullenly, "It was a mistake."

Which, truly, it was. We were too close in the doorway for me to do what I wanted to do, which was to pull her stupid healthy hair so hard that it separated from her stupid healthy scalp and stopped mocking me. So I went for her neck, thinking that if her lungs didn't have any air, she'd at least stop whining.

Debra, pointing to nonexistent marks on her neck, wailed, "She could have killed me!"

I thought, *No. I have small hands and my position provided very little leverage. Had I wanted you dead, I would have doctored your Yoplait with antifreeze and wiped off the fingerprints.* The mere fact that such an answer had come so easily to me meant it probably wasn't going to strengthen my case.

"We're probably going to expel you for this," the vice principal said, her serious tone at odds with the glee snapping in her eyes. "But first, I want to get your mother in here."

My mind raced. My mother didn't need this. My mother was currently at her office, vomiting and trying to work. If my mother showed up at school in her beige wig and her gray skin this nitwit functionary would know she was sick, the secret would be out, and it would be my fault.

I turned to Debra. I worked up some tears. I sniffled, "God, Debra, I'm so sorry. I was just trying to goof around with you. I knew you had lived through this nightmare and I just . . ." I sobbed a bit more, for emphasis, "just wanted to make you laugh by roughhousing. It was all just a terrible, thoughtless mistake."

I wiped my eyes and carried on a bit. Debra, puzzled at this turn of events, patted my hand. The vice principal played with her pen in a way that suggested she wanted a cigarette. Debra turned to the vice principal.

"She just wanted to make me laugh by roughhousing," she said sweetly. "It was all a terrible, thoughtless mistake."

Did I say I despised her mindless parroting of what people said to her? I was so very wrong. It was her best quality. The vice principal frowned. She could continue to prosecute me, but it wouldn't work nearly as well without the victim's tearful testimony. I smiled at Debra through my tears and hugged her, careful to avoid touching her neck or her hair. She packed up and went off to blindly excel in another class. I smiled slightly differently at the vice principal.

"Is that it?" I asked.

"For the moment," she said, grudgingly. "Just . . ."

She stopped. She had gone from nearly getting rid of me to sending me to fifth period with a late pass. She needed to warn me about something.

"Just don't touch people."

I picked up my backpack and leaned across the table. "Don't worry," I said, calmly. "I don't plan on getting close to anyone."

Ask for Flaco

ONE WEEKEND MORNING, I FOUND ALICE IN HER BEDROOM paging through a children's book about the body. She said dreamily, "I'd like to see a heart." Choosing the easy and obvious reply, I pointed at the page where she was reading and said, "There you go."

She shook her head and sighed, "No." Then, tracing the aorta with her finger, she added, "In real life." The voice was soft and dreamy, with a tone she might someday use to describe the captain of the water-polo team. But right now it seemed that Alice had a crush on the cardiovascular system. She then turned to me and said pleadingly, "Can I have a heart? A real human one? To dissect?"

I answered with the classic, "We'll see," which is another way to say "I thank God for your ability to be distracted by the modern age." What I failed to understand was that her need to see a human heart was a need to glance at our collective mortality in a small and measured way. This might be put aside briefly by Polly Pockets, but it certainly wasn't going to be assuaged unless Ms. Pockets suddenly developed ventricles. Within weeks, I went from, "Medical school is chock-full of human hearts, so work on your multiplication tables" to "Amazon doesn't have human hearts, sweetie. It seems like they should, and I'd get you one if they did, but they don't; however, there's always medical school so please go work on your multiplication tables."

One day, after Alice mentioned yet again how nice it would be to find a bloody human heart in her Easter basket, the inner voice that sends me off on idiotic adventures cleared its throat and spoke up. "You know," it announced, "she's showing an interest in science, and you're shutting it down. Either you find her a heart to cut open or you risk her joining a squad of cheerleaders who trade sexual favors with science teachers in exchange for passing grades. Your choice."

I sat her down and told her the news. Yes, I would get her a real heart. She gasped and interlaced her fingers under her chin in a perfect display of innocent girlish delight, her mind racing toward hacking away at oozing crimson chambers. But, I continued, it couldn't be a human heart. The federal government frowns on selling organs to civilians. Also, grave robbing. I was prepared to deliver either a pig's heart or a cow's heart. As her personal organ shopper, I noted that a pig's heart was closer in size and configuration to a human heart but I advocated the cow's heart, which, being larger, allowed for a wider margin of error.

[Having seen Alice attempt to butter a hard roll and section an apple, I knew we needed all the margin we could get.]

I figured I was now out of the woods, effort-wise. I was no longer facing a trip to some dimly lit alley behind the city morgue, exchanging unmarked bills with a loan-laden med student. Instead, I could head to the nearest butcher shop, sing out "One heart, please! And don't stint on the veins!", and we'd be set. I couldn't remember ever seeing a heart at a butcher's shop, but what do I know? I'm a vegetarian. I slither through that section of the market covering my eyes in the same way one does when passing certain magazine racks. In either case, we're talking about body parts dedicated to bring pleasure to someone who isn't me.

Here's a fact: When you ask for a cow's heart at a butcher shop they look at you funny. They look at you funny in the upscale market where the lamb comes in its own tankini and matching flip-flops. They look at you funny in the neighborhood store whose street-facing sign boasts, "Tripe and Head Cheese—Half Off." They look at you funny in places that specialize in the meats of certain countries known for the paucity of food and the culinary inventiveness they apply to every single part of the animal; cuisines with holiday menus that proudly include earlobe and hoof stew with a side of pan-roasted nose hair. Even *these* butchers looked at me funny after I asked for a cow's heart. They typically said something that translated as "ew." It seems not a single culture represented in Los Angeles, a place with more languages than the United Nations, ever looked at a cow's heart and thought, *Yum! All for me!*

What all these butchers did have in common was a belief that I celebrated some religion you hope your new neighbors don't. A typical conversation went like this:

"Do you have a cow's heart?"

"A what?"

"A cow's heart."

"A cow part? You mean, like a steak?"

"H . . . eart. Heart. Big muscle, squeezes blood."

At which point, the butcher would lean over the counter and, to a person, cautiously inquire, "Is this for your church or something?"

Yes, you caught me. I'm a high priestess in a blood-worshipping cult. You can spot us by our mom haircuts and sensible sedans. Until now, I assumed sheer suburban dreariness rendered me harmless on sight but this didn't seem to work in the world of meat. I decided if Alice was so eager to see the dark recesses of a mammal's heart she could damn well see the dark recesses of a butcher shop, so I invited her to join the quest. I figured that dragging a small child on my hunt for raw flesh would surely present a less sinister-looking front than my traveling alone. Wasn't I just gloriously mistaken.

Imagine you are a butcher. Now imagine a mother and a small child walk up to your counter, the mother prods her daughter slightly, and the little girl pipes up with, "Please, do you have a cow's heart for sale?" while her mother beams down at her. The mother is either smiling in pride at her daughter's good manners and articulation, or she is smiling in delightful anticipation of her child's first blood ritual. Maybe if you explain to them that you don't sell cow hearts, they will leave. Or maybe the mother will smile more broadly and announce, "What a lucky girl you are, your first blood shall be freshly spilled from a real live butcher!"

Butchers tend to be physically large men. Alice's and my request caused no fewer than three of them to dart for the back of their shops and refuse to come out.

Finally, one butcher decided we weren't dangerous as much as really, really strange. He took pity on us and told us the news: we might possibly be able to buy a bunch of cow's hearts—

which are sold to pet-food companies in volume—but not just one. Even if we did find someone who would sell us a single heart, it would be cut in half—a regulation that had something to do with mad cow disease. Had I been a reasonable person, I would have thought something like, *Hey, after nearly two months of butcher-bothering, I'll take what I can get. Half a heart is better than blah blah blah . . .*

Luckily, the part of my brain that usually runs things vetoed the smaller, more reasonable voice in my head, and insisted I get a whole cow's heart or be found wanting in my child's eyes. I pestered my new butcher buddy further and, after much pleading on my part and pointing to Alice and wailing pitifully, "It's for the child. It's for all our future cardiologists!", he finally slid me a phone number. I was to call a butcher shop located in a traditionally Mexican neighborhood in Los Angeles and I was to ask for Flaco. I was to clarify that I didn't want Flaquito, but Flaco—Flaquito would be of no help and might possibly turn us all in to the Food and Drug Administration. If I used the name of this butcher as a discreet reference, Flaco might possibly be able to hook me up. I thanked my new friend and promised to eat the paper containing Flaco's phone number once the transaction was complete.

It took several phone calls to actually connect with Flaco. They kept putting Flaquito on the phone, but I was too paranoid to leave my name and number. Finally, one Saturday morning, I got the elusive Flaco. The conversation went like this:

QUINN: Is this Flaco?

FLACO: You want Flaquito?

QUINN: NO! I mean, no. Ronnie said to call you. He said he told you what I'm looking to buy.

FLACO: Yeah, I can get it.

QUINN: I don't want it cut. You can get it uncut, right?

FLACO: Yeah, for a little extra. Give me a week. Come to the store, around back, but don't talk to anyone but me.

Apparently, the government was only monitoring phone calls for terrorist activities that week and not interested in major drug trafficking because, so far, no team of machine-gun toting federal agents has broken into my house.

It was late February when Alice first indicated a need for a heart to touch and call her very own. By August her passion remained undimmed. I decided not to tell her about our rendezvous with Flaco until the very morning of the pickup; I suspected that if you're at ballet class and your daughter suddenly blurts out, "I can't wait three days until we're cutting open a real heart!" the other mothers stop offering to share hairpins.

Saturday morning arrived. The air drooped around us in the stale, grimy oven blast that makes Los Angeles natives wonder why anyone moves here. I hustled Alice through Saturday's breakfast and getting dressed. As I steered her toward the garage she asked, "Ballet class?"

"No."

"Karate class?"

"No."

"Gymnastics?"

"No."

"Horseback riding?"

"No."

Yes, it's possible we needed to cut back on her schedule. "Actually," I said, in the breathless tone of the emcee announcing who was to be first runner-up and who was now Miss Universe, "We're going to pick up your cow's heart!"

The scream of delight was gratifying. We both flew into the car. Of course, that was the last time we traveled faster than a walk for the next hour. To get to the neighborhood where our hookup was to occur we needed to take the freeway. It was Saturday morning, not even 9:00 a.m. yet, but the freeway was packed solid. Being a native, I decided it was people trying to get to another freeway, which would take them to the beach, mercifully in the opposite direction. This logic worked only until we passed that juncture and the traffic grew worse.

Okay, I thought grimly, there was an accident somewhere up ahead so, I turned on the AM news-radio station. Nothing. If there was an accident up ahead, it was one of those super-secret, invisible black-ops accidents that aren't reported. I sank a little farther into my seat and entered into the driver's version of hibernation; my breathing slowed, my metabolism dropped, I prepared to be out of commission until spring when I would emerge from the freeway hungry and irritable. But being in traffic wasn't all that bad. The car wasn't uncomfortable and the kid was reading.

Suddenly, either I entered menopause or the temperature in the car went up by thirty degrees. I put my hand over the vent. The air blasting out had gone from soothingly cool to hellishly hot. My car had recently entered its dementia years and had taken to periodically forgetting how to air-condition. Our trustworthy and supremely competent mechanic had pronounced the situations "weird," "too expensive to fix," "possibly not fixable," and "a big pain in the ass." While we tried to figure out the best way to repair it without compromising Alice's college plans, he suggested I switch off the air-conditioning whenever it got mulish. I felt virtuous in a smaller carbon-footprint way. I could simply roll down the windows and let the breeze do its work.

However, a breeze requires two things: air and movement. Air we had, smelly and dust-infused as it was. But with the car going no more than four miles an hour in fifty-yard spurts, the interior quickly took on the comfort profile of a convection oven. Alice was a resilient passenger focused on her book, but after a few minutes she mournfully informed me, "I'm really warm."

I reached back and patted her sweaty knee with my soaking-wet hand. "I know, baby," I said, trying to toggle the air-conditioning back into self-awareness. "Just read and try to ignore it."

Maybe not the dumbest statement I have ever uttered, but not far from the top. First of all, it had to be over a hundred de-grees in the car and only a desert tortoise could have been blasé about the heat. Second, encouraging her to keep reading only guaranteed that it was going to stop being a morning about the cardiovascular system and start being a morning about the di-gestive system. Within a few minutes, when she said, "I'm going to stop reading now. I think I'm feeling a little motion sickness," my own stomach sank. Alice has such a fear of vomiting that by the time she finally admits it's not entirely out of the realm of possibility that she's feeling a bit nauseated, anyone else would be screaming, "BUCKET!" I drove with one hand and waved what little fresh air I could generate toward her face while men-tally scanning the car for anything we could use as a receptacle. I remembered a plastic bag in the trunk, which, had we been moving at all, would have been impossible, but lucky us, we were again at a complete stop.

I raced out, grabbed the bag, and got back in the car. With a dart of joy, I saw the next exit was ours. "Breathe through your mouth and think about Pomeranian puppies," I caroled in hysterical delight, "because we're almost there!"

With a deft vehicular sideways lunge across three lanes of snarled traffic, we were liberated. The sudden movement of the car caused the inner-car temperature to jump down to a bracing ninety-five degrees. The air-conditioning sputtered back to life. Alice went from chalk-white to sort of a dusky green. I chose to view all these things as good news.

The butcher's shop was a few minutes from the off-ramp on a sweltering boulevard mostly dedicated to stores selling handmade tortillas, illegal immigration cards, and Lotto tickets. We parked around the back and sidled in. The store was shabby but clean, which pleased me for no especially good reason; did hacking an organ to pieces in one's backyard become more wholesome if the dealer's nails were scrubbed?

The man behind the counter said, "Can I help you?" As I said, "I'm looking for Flaco and not Flaquito," Alice interrupted with, "Do you have a trash can?" in a somewhat desperate and clenched tone.

Puzzled at her intensity, he pointed her to the standing trash can at the end of the counter, to which she ran. She opened the swinging lid and vomited copiously. We are not a pat-my-head-while-I-puke people. We are more a you-must-have-something-better-to-do-than-touch-me-right-now people, so I left her to her work. I turned to the counterman and smiled as brightly as I could while feeling sweat pool in my waistband and my bra. He said, softly, "I'm Flaco?" His mouth said that. His eyes said, "What bet did I lose to get the two of you?"

I leaned over the counter and said under my breath, "I think you have something for me. An . . . organ?" I thought it sounded both enigmatic and possibly obscene, but he shrugged and said, "Oh, the heart. Hold on."

I was oddly disappointed. After all the drama it had taken to get here, I had hoped the theme to *Mission Impossible* would start playing from the walls. Alice had finished vomiting. Some color returned to her face and she was hopping around in excitement over the transaction. Flaco came out, carrying something about the size of a soccer ball, marbled in shades of red, pink, and beige. It was in a plastic bag, but the bag appeared to have developed a leak. He plopped the bag on the counter, where it made an unsettling wet sound. We all stared at it. I felt I had to say something.

"Well, that's . . . big," I observed, because I didn't think "organy" was a word.

Flaco poked at it professionally. "That's mostly fat," he noted. "The heart's about half that big."

"Let's go," Alice implored, "I want to get home and dissect . . . wait!" She dashed back to the trash can and vomited again. I was so pleased we had forgone our typically light weekday breakfast this morning and gone with the bagels and cream cheese.

Flaco and I both watched her vomit for a second and then turned back to the moist mound on the counter. He said warningly, "You know you can't eat this, right?" and I noted how, in the eyes of the butchering class, I had progressed from organ-worshipping cult member to organ-worshipping stew maker.

I guess Alice's repeated vomiting suggested I took some delight in feeding my daughter the inedible.

"So," I said, "how much?"

Flaco thought for a second and said, "Six bucks?" as if it still seemed ludicrous to him that I was insisting on paying for his offal. I handed over a sweat-saturated five and a single, which he slid directly into his pocket. The financials taken care of, this heart truly mine, he asked briskly, "So, where's your cooler?"

Cooler, what the hell is a cooler? Wait, calm down. That must be some new slang word for car. I said knowingly, "Oh, it's out back."

He stared at me, I stared at him. The heart oozed at both of us. He said slowly, "Then, bring it in, so I can put the heart in it."

Oh. Not a car. A *cooler*. The kind that holds ice. Crap.

"I don't . . . I mean, I do . . . but it's at home . . . have one," I stammered. To distract us from my blathering, I yelled in a loving way at Alice, "Honey, are you done vomiting?"

She answered me by sidling up to the heart and poking at it curiously with her index finger. The bag released a little blood onto the counter. I said firmly, "Stop poking at your heart, sweetie. It will be less disgusting in the car if you let it congeal a little." I then took a moment to consider whether that exact phrase had ever been spoken before in the entire history of language.

Flaco raised his eyebrows. "You have a long trip home?"

I said, "No," without any hesitation. Compared to driving from here to Shreveport, Louisiana, our trip wasn't long at all.

"You should be okay," Flaco said, obviously counting the seconds until he was done with my family. "Just keep the air-conditioning on high and go straight home."

"Our air-conditioning isn't . . ." Alice blurted out, but I felt we had drawn Flaco far enough into our sordid lives so I gently pinched her shoulder.

"Alice," I purred. "Do you want to help carry the heart to the car?" Her yelp of delight would have pleased any parent on Christmas morning.

I kept the air-conditioning on high all the way home, and it managed to drool out coolish air every few minutes. Alice kept the heart in her lap and petted its fat. We got home, changed into clothing that wouldn't be compromised by random blots of clotting blood, found Consort's X-ACTO kit, took the heart into the backyard, and commenced to cutting. I propped a text-book picture of a cow's heart against the wall of her sandbox and braced it with a My Little Pony. The cat circled us impatiently, puzzled as to why we were playing with her dinner.

Historically, scientists have been both fascinated and mistaken about the true purpose of the heart. The Egyptians thought it was the source of wisdom, personality, emotions, memory, and the soul. Aristotle thought it was the seat of intelligence, motion, and sensation; he described it as a three-chambered organ that was the "center of vitality" in the body and the "source of nerves." Galen thought it was second in importance to the liver, which makes me imagine the major viscera erupting into a hair-pulling girl fight over who gets to be the Organ Queen. By the Middle Ages, enlightened anatomists understood its primary function was as a circulating pump but didn't give up the secondary idea of the heart being the source of all human emotions until well into the seventeenth century.

Modern scientists agree that a heart is nothing more than a miraculously well-engineered device. It is an organ of vital importance, to be sure, but it is not integral to the emotional life of its owner. On that scorching afternoon, as the sun baked dribbles of blood into the patio and I examined small chunks of cardiac tissue under a borrowed microscope with my rapturously curious child, I would have been forced to argue otherwise. This heart, cut from an anonymous cow in a feedlot in central California, made its two new owners very happy.

Later that night, Consort and I were putting Alice to bed. She was entertaining her father with stories of us flicking veins at one another. Because he's a very nice man and because he wanted to steer her away from that anecdote, he said, "Sounds like you had a very good time. I think you owe your mother a hug and a thank you."

She leapt from her bed into my arms. My lovely girl, my wonderful kid, this blazingly clever individual hugged me with all her strength. She then whispered into my ear, "Thank you, Mommy. Now we need lungs."

A Big Mean Pair of Scissors

I GREW UP IN THE HILLS ABOVE WEST HOLLYWOOD. THIS neighborhood competes with the Castro District in San Francisco, New York's Fire Island, and a reunion of Liberace's chauffeurs as being the gayest place on earth. In our canyon there were about a hundred houses and four children. Every Halloween, my mother and I would make a lonely trek through the neighborhood where, at any given house, my "Trick or Treat!" would produce a man dressed as either Maria Callas or Marilyn in *The Seven Year Itch*. For a long moment, he would stare at me in confusion then say something like, "Everyone, come here and look! It's a child!" At which point more men in festive regalia would crowd the doorway and goggle at me for a bit, apparently having forgotten there was another segment of the population allowed one night a year to wear something ridiculously bright and sparkly out in public without recrimination.

Having cooed over my small size and fancy outfit there would be a flurry of whispered, "What the hell do we give her?" Typically, my Halloween haul would include a few Godiva chocolates, a rhinestone brooch, and lip gloss. One well-meaning young man, after zipping away from the door and a much hurried conversation with his friends, came back with one of those mini-bottles of scotch you get on an airplane. He waved it at my mother and said, "Do you think she'd like it? I know she can't drink it, but it's got a pretty label." I was in full agreement about the teeny image of the white stag, but my mother got traditional all of a sudden and decided her five-year-old didn't need any oak-distilled beverages quite yet.

Even without Halloween, I always liked the men in our neighborhood. I had every intention of growing up to be a gay man in the West Hollywood hills. They had gorgeous clothing, gorgeous houses, gorgeous boyfriends, and gorgeous dogs. From my bedroom I could gaze out across the canyon and observe our neighbors' parties. Everyone seemed young and beautiful and inebriated with life. From up here, life was the eternal golden Sunday afternoon of a three-day weekend, a dreamy time and place where a small girl and a lot of grown men never sensed how cold things were about to get.

Somewhere not long after I turned fourteen, I saw one of the longer-time residents out walking his dog. I hadn't seen him in many weeks and I was shocked. He had lost twenty pounds at least, and there were coal-black rings under his eyes. Something told me not to ask. He was dead within a month. He was the first person I knew who died of AIDS. I don't remember who the second and third were, because they started going so quickly. I stopped noticing the sound of the ambulance racing up our hill.

AIDS was a big mean pair of scissors in West Hollywood. There was no AZT in the early eighties, no immune cocktails. There was only brutally efficient speed. The person you chatted with in his front yard in March would look tired by May, had friends walking his dog by September, received around-the-clock care by November, and was memorialized at a service before Christmas. We lost about one out of four neighbors in less than five years.

These dazzling and boyish men became all too adult overnight. One neighbor I knew pretty well nursed his long-time boyfriend through the last terrible months. After a couple of years, he met and fell in love again but his new boyfriend was already sick and didn't last out the summer. Finally, our friend, sick himself and maybe too worn out from a half decade of caring for friends and lovers, succumbed to the virus. I sat on our porch and watched as his friends packed up his house as the Realtor put up the "For Sale" sign. I made a decision: I was going to stop AIDS. I was eighteen, I had no medical training and a habit of covering my eyes and squealing when they inserted a fake IV on hospital dramas, but these were incidental details I could overcome. I was going to stop AIDS.

As it turned out, the workers at the front lines of the battle against AIDS didn't fall to their knees and scream "HUZZAH! She's arrived!" when I called AIDS Project Los Angeles. What they said was, "We need help in the office. Can you file?"

I sulked a bit. I can file, but where's the life-saving potential in that? I asked if there was anything else.

"If you can cook, we always need help in the home-care kitchen."

Technically, I could cook, inasmuch as I could heat food in a pan. But since I assumed the point of the food was to make sick people actually feel better, I didn't see this as a perfect match for my skills.

"Anything else?"

I could hear him flipping through pages. "Oh, you're in

luck," he finally said, "there's a hotline training class starting this week."

"Hotline?"

"Yeah, we have a national hotline for information and support. It can be anything from finding a local clinic for people to get tested to helping someone who's just gotten a positive test result to . . . everything, really."

The part of my brain that is activated upon exposure to genuine philanthropy was flooded with endorphins. I would work the hotline. I would give people valuable information. I would be useful. I did a little dance around my room while maintaining what I hoped was a mature and altruistic tone of voice. "Heck," I said, "I can do that."

I don't know why I thought I could work on a hotline. Most of the people calling the hotline had questions related to sexual practices or intravenous drug use, and I had a complete lack of firsthand experience in both categories. I might as well have been volunteering for a jet aircraft maintenance hotline. Luckily for those callers who were going to need me to actually know what the hell I was talking about, I had several weeks of training before they'd let me answer a phone. In a class of several dozen, I was one of three women. I was the youngest trainee by eight years. I brought several sharpened pencils and a notebook with "Hotline" carefully printed across the front. One of these facts made the teacher pick on me from day one.

He was gorgeous—a six-foot-five-inch-tall black man with the effortless grace of an athlete and the humor and affect of a very tall and very tan Bette Midler. His job was to educate us, support us, and keep us from freaking out. At some point during the first week, he decided I needed the most educating, the least support, and I would look the funniest freaking out. Near the end of every class, he would bring one of us up front to role-play a hotline call, with him as the caller and the student assuming his or her role as hotline advisor. Of course, being all enthusiasm and no experience, I was summoned to the front of the class four times out of five. I was a golden retriever puppy taking on Chernobyl.

One night he, as the caller, asked me, the hotline counselor, if "felching was safe." Never having heard the word, but sensing from the way the gay men in the class had just fallen out of their chairs screaming in laughter that this was another "Get Quinn" moment, I responded in my flattest, most nonjudgmental tone, "I'm going to need a little more information. What, exactly, is felching?"

The few men who had crawled back into their seats, pawing the tears out of their eyes, went rolling off again. My instructor, as my new telephonic friend, explained to me what this was. His depiction was vivid, unexpected, and involved little in the way of subtlety. I sat straighter in my chair and forced a picture of kittens playing with a ball of yarn into my head as I explained that no, felching was greatly unsafe, and probably couldn't be made safe without seriously compromising whatever entertainment value it held for the participants.

I persevered. After forty hours of class, I had a working knowledge of the major and most of the minor sexual habits of the North American Homo erectus. I had also developed the ability to work needle-cleaning protocol into casual conversation. We, as a class, were ready to serve, but the teacher had one final lesson to impart. He leaned against a chair, crossing his arms and his endless legs, and looked at us deeply. "Four friends of mine and I sat in an apartment and started what has become this organization. I'm the only one left. I don't know why I'm still alive, but I do know why I'm still able to work here. I go to the gym every morning. I put on my Walkman, and I don't talk to anyone, and I don't think about this place. You went through this because you want to help, but don't overdo it. The hotline takes more out of you than you know." He then lectured us on the symptoms of burnout, which I carefully wrote down in my "Hotline" notebook so I could more effectively monitor my classmates in the months to come. I was going to be fine, but I could tell that some of these people weren't going to be able to keep things in proper balance.

My first shift was on a Saturday morning. I sat at a cubicle with a three-inch-thick binder in front of me, which represented the sum total of medical information and support for AIDS patients in the entire United States. An inch of that represented California and another inch New York. The final inch was the other forty-eight states with a page or two for Canada. Within minutes, the phone rang and I answered, "AIDS hotline, how can I help you?" with only the tiniest quaver, all the while thinking *Please don't be crying, please don't be crying, please be something I can answer.*

A brisk male voice said, "Hi, I need to get tested in Orange County, California." I nearly giggled in delight but checked the impulse, deciding this was not the image I wanted to present. I gave him his testing options, wished him luck, and hung up. Eighty percent of my calls on any given shift were looking for testing locations, the only variables being what day I worked.

On the weekends, there was a steady stream of "Yeah, I had a teensy bit too much tequila last night, and I never do this, but . . . how long do I have to wait to get tested?"

I labeled those calls, as a group, "Oops." Subheadings included:

#1. Agave.

#2. Cannabis sativa.

#3. Ecstasy.

#4. Being super-mad at your boyfriend for still describing you to his mother as his roommate.

#5. He was really hot.

If I worked a weekday, I'd get calls from suburban moms who had watched a documentary the previous night about how AIDS was about to inundate the heterosexual community, and who had spent the entire night obsessing over their college boyfriend who, in retrospect, might have liked musical theater just a *little too much*. Telling them how unlikely they were to have been exposed to AIDS in the early seventies at Iowa State would ease their fears, but they'd still want a local test site, which I would gladly provide.

About fifteen percent of the calls were the *Misfit Toys*. For these people, the hotline served as a form of solace and an unending source of entertainment. Thanks to our 1-800 number, they could pick up a phone and talk endlessly about their deeply held suspicions about how AIDS could be contracted from houseplants, or escalators, or doorknobs. Doorknob Guy was a frequent caller, and getting a new hotline volunteer was like Christmas and his birthday rolled into one. The new volunteer could be coaxed into a forty-five-minute trip down the rabbit hole where AIDS patients had sneezed into their hand—that sneeze carrying a trace of blood—then touched a doorknob and left AIDS viruses writhing and throbbing, waiting for their next victim.

The first time I got him, I spent almost half an hour before hanging up the phone, exhausted and headachy from trying to explain epidemiology to a lunatic, only to hear the phone in the cubicle next to mine ring. The phones rang in order and I just knew it was Doorknob Guy, fat and sassy from our conversation and hungry for a new victim. The volunteer next to me, a sea-soned vet of several months, picked up the phone and said, "AIDS hotline, how can I help you?" He listened for a few sec-onds and then said waggishly, "Sweetie, it depends on what you do with that doorknob," then hung up sharply and turned to me, a pleasant expression on his face.

"And *that's* how you handle Doorknob Guy," he said with finality.

But I would take a dozen hardware fetishists over the mas-turbators. Those calls would always begin in a routine way, with some guy asking a question like, "How does AIDS trans-mit through sexual intercourse?" or "What's a safer way to have sex?" I'd start into my prepared pitch when, slowly, it would dawn on me that I was hearing panting and a faint slapping sound. Thanks to my hotline training, I knew what I had to do. In as prim a voice as I could manage, and hoping I was some-how reminding him of his mother (unless that added to the whole experience, in which case, no), I would say, "Excuse me, but are you masturbating?" I don't know why I had to ask but it was protocol. I mean, it wasn't as if he was going to say, "No, but I could understand the confusion. I just like to shampoo my pet otter when I make phone calls." In most cases, once I suggested he was using me for other than completely informational purposes, the caller would hang up, but one gentleman exploded with a heartfelt and grateful, "I SURE AM!" As a person who craves being of service, I guess this should have thrilled me on some level, but somehow it fell flat.

Other than that, hotline volunteering was great. Not every phone call was productive; some were fairly unpleasant, thanks to the percentage of the population whose own version of Jesus hated us very much and needed us to know that. Nonetheless, each shift generated at least one call where I could tell myself, "I helped him." One caller had tested positive the day before and while he wasn't really surprised, he was kind of sad and terrified and inasmuch as he had to be in his brother's wedding that afternoon, would I just talk to him? I spent an hour walking him through his medical and support options in his state, which were slightly better than average. We talked about his friends, his hobbies, and his plans. I couldn't change his HIV status, but I did help to take the hollow sound out of his voice. At the end of the phone call, he said, sighing, "Oh, I'd love to keep chatting, but I have to go put on a tuxedo now. I'm the best man, you know." I grinned, hoping he could hear it, and said, "You certainly are."

Within weeks, I'd grown polished and confident. I was a seasoned veteran. Nothing I heard surprised me. I was the one slamming shut Doorknob Guy to the wonder of the newer volunteers. When we were in training, my mentor explained how some counselors resisted talking to the heroin addicts because of a perception they wouldn't change their behavior and, besides, they weren't the most lucid conversationalists. I had enough experience in the trenches that I could state with authority that not only did I *not* mind junkies, I preferred them to speed freaks. Neither group was going to change behavior anytime soon, but at least the junkies were quiet and let you tell them how to clean their needles; they didn't start screaming about how the police were crawling in under the air-conditioner. I was never at a loss for words, never judgmental, never shocked. Every week, there were more people wanting to get tested, more people looking for health care after they'd tested positive, and more people calling for the list of mortuaries who would take people who had died of AIDS. In six months, the call volume doubled.

During this time I developed a vocational understanding of what it must be like to be a priest. Not only was I giving counsel on matters for which I had no practical experience, I was spending six hours a week hearing the most insane, or tragic, or funny, or all-of-the-above narratives and *I couldn't tell anyone*. It would have been unethical to share these stories with my friends, however scrubbed of personal details. But what really kept me on the straight and narrow was the suitable anxiety that my blabbing a hotline story in a restaurant would only guarantee the subject would be sitting in the booth behind me—*exactly* the sort of thing that happens to me on a regular basis. And even if I could talk about the callers, I was eighteen. Not one of my friends would want to hear stories from the AIDS hotline. I could imagine the conversation. Over dinner, a friend would dig into the guacamole and ask innocently, "So, Quinn, what's new with you?"

"Nothing much," I'd yell over the restaurant noise. "I got

new shoes. Joined a gym. Oh, and I helped this guy deal with the American Embassy in London so he could ship his lover's body home. And don't get me started about AIDS-friendly crematoria in Maryland. I don't understand why they're so obsessed about bodily fluids when everyone knows that the inside of the oven gets to well over fourteen hundred degrees, and no retrovirus could survive that."

I'd look at my friend, her face aghast, a chip frozen in space halfway between the guacamole bowl and her mouth. That's when I'd think: *Oh, right. That was my outside voice.* At which point I would follow up with a feeble, "They were pumps. The shoes, I mean."

I worked the phones, I heard stuff, and I kept it to myself. There were group stress-reduction sessions for the hotline volunteers—the only people who might appreciate firsthand gossip about crematoria in Maryland—but I never bothered to go. I was helping. I didn't need help.

The call came on a quiet weekday morning. The caller was sobbing so hard it took her a few minutes to collect herself enough to explain what she needed. She wasn't calling for herself. She was calling for a friend, a sorority sister. The entire sorority had gone, en masse, to get tested, and they got their results this morning. Her friend, eighteen and with one sexual partner, had tested positive. My brain raced. Was this a hoax? It didn't matter if it was; I had to treat it seriously either way. But if it was a hoax, this girl needed an agent. My inner lie detector said it was probably legit, the only question being whether this "friend" was, in fact, my caller. I asked what state she was in and when she told me, I nearly burst into tears myself. She was calling from the Southern state with only one page of medical and psychological support in place—actually half a page—and nothing specifically for women. I gave her what I had, and tried to calm her down enough to see this wasn't an immediate death sentence—although, at that time, a positive test wasn't exactly a reason to start putting money into your IRA.

The call ended. I hung up, and then I stood up. I said to no one in particular, "I'm cutting out early," and I left. I got to the parking lot, sat in my car, and switched the radio off because I couldn't stand the noise. I then switched it back on because the silence was overwhelming. My brain couldn't find anywhere to land. I had started working at APLA so I could help the gay community in which I had grown up and the addicts who weren't capable of shaking an addiction that was going to kill them unless they took care of themselves. This was the first phone call where it occurred to me that the *them* in the AIDS epidemic might look a lot like *me*. I couldn't save my neighbors or my fellow human beings, but what kind of an ass was I that it finally broke my heart when the caller looked like the person I saw in the mirror?

I came back for my next shift, but I wasn't much good. Every time the phone rang, I'd let it go an extra ring, wondering if it would be another girl my age. I snapped, "Do you *mind*?" at two volunteers who were chatting while waiting for a call. I started not showing up for shifts. I no longer believed I could help.

I stopped in to see the hotline supervisor and mumbled my complaints. The job wasn't any fun, or I wasn't good at it, and it was because I got this one call. I had been fine until this one stupid call, which made me feel itchy, sad, and really angry. Besides, everyone else kept talking when I was trying to take a call and no one ever made a fresh pot of coffee, which sucked even freshly made, and it would have been fine if I just hadn't gotten this one call. Finished, I slumped farther down in my seat. My mentor sighed deeply.

"How many support meetings did you attend?" he asked.

"Uh," I stammered, "you mean here?"

"So, none. Lost enthusiasm for the job. Irritable. No longer confident in your ability, right? That college girl may have been your last straw, but it's burnout, Quinn. Remember?"

I mentally flew back to our last day of class. Oh. Yeah.

"You're totally right," I said, humbled. "What should I do?"

"Take a month off. See if your heart is in it after that. You've been volunteering how long?"

I thought. "Six months." It seemed longer.

"You made it about the average."

I thought for a second and said guiltily, "There's really nothing wrong with the coffee."

"No," he said reflectively. "The coffee is awful. Wouldn't you think a bunch of gay men could chip in and get the good stuff?"

I took off a month, and then two. And then it was pilot season, the actor's busy season. I told myself I had to be available for auditions at any time, conveniently forgetting that auditions came along for me about as often as panda births. Three months later, as pilot season ended and I was still gainfully unemployed, I didn't go back. I beat myself up plenty over that. A few more neighbors were sick, a couple had died, and I still didn't go back. I didn't help because I couldn't help. A teenage girl with a notebook full of phone numbers wasn't going to change a damn thing. I brooded.

A month or so later, I was standing in line at the bank in West Hollywood ahead of two trim young men. From their chatting, I deduced they were here on vacation to enjoy all the pleasures West Hollywood had to offer. Apparently, one had made a less-than-completely-safe decision the night before. Kamikazes had been involved. His friend said, "Y'all should totally go get tested today. You know, to be safe and shit like that."

I turned and leapt in. "You have to wait six to eight weeks for HIV to show up in your blood." The men, understandably somewhat confused at having accidentally walked into a health-education movie starring a teenager in sweatpants and an ancient T-shirt advertising the band The English Beat, gaped at me. I continued, "Are you going home before then?"

They looked at each other and nodded.

"Where do you live?"

The kamikaze drinker said, "Roanoke? . . . Virginia?" as if I might deny him that.

"There's a testing center there, but I can't remember the name." I grabbed a deposit slip and the bank's chained-up pen and wrote out the number of the hotline. "Call this number. Ask for the Roanoke testing location."

I paused for a second, and then decided to really make this conversation memorable for them. I leaned in and said confidentially, "If I may ask, what did you guys do that worries you?"

He and his friend looked at one another again. It was a credit to how weird this whole conversation had been that neither man took a swing at me. The kamikaze drinker leaned in and whispered something. I said brightly, "Oh, that's usually pretty low risk, but it never hurts to check. And from now on, play safe, okay?"

They looked at one another, at me, and at the sheet of paper I was offering. A bank teller waved me up.

"Okay, thanks," the friend said, taking the number.

"Happy to help," I smiled. As I approached the teller, my step had a bit more bounce.

Crunch

MY DAUGHTER HAD MOVED UP TO A NEW LEVEL IN HER gymnastics. Alice was now the smallest girl in a gymnasium filled with highly motivated young athletes sporting a worrying display of elastic bandages, smelly liniment, and game faces. No longer was she being instructed by an angel-faced ingénue with an inclination to reward hard work with hugs and stickers. Her new coach had a talent for the disapproving snort and a barked "Do it again." The new coach's real passion in life was abdominal strength. Each practice began with crunches. Each practice ended with sit-ups. Sit-ups were the punishment for chatting in line waiting for the beam. Within a day of her first class, Alice began to learn about the mysterious world of muscle pain. Her stomach hurt, she informed me one morning as we were prepared to leave for school.

"Not inside," she said. "Outside." She tapped approximately where her liver was.

"Oh," I said distractedly, continuing to search the house for my keys, glasses, purse, iPod, and the dog's eye drops. "That's from all the sit-ups you did yesterday. It will get better."

Pretty early on, Consort and I realized Alice was going to be an only child. Also, she was going to be the only child of parents who weren't in their twenties when she was born. I've known many parents who fit this description, and too many of them behave as if theirs was the first child ever born, too delicate and refined for this hostile world. One family I knew was still carrying their fourth-grade daughter into school every day, her pelvis on her father's hip, her legs brushing the floor. Another mother I knew liked to hide in the bushes near her son's school, watching him interact with the world. Whenever he played any game more boisterous than loitering, she would get the panicky look of someone who wished to shove her child back into the womb.

To my way of thinking, my job as a parent was to treat Alice with the same deep and profound love as any mother, but with the Oh-there's-plenty-more-where-that-came-from attitude of parents with multiple offspring. This would afford us all a dose of healthy separateness and an inoculation from my own special blend of crazy—I didn't want to find myself hiding under my child's bed in a freshman dormitory. One symptom of this artificial composure occurs when Alice voices a physical complaint and there's no bone protruding, blood spurting, or her temperature isn't disturbing the air above her head in visible waves. In such cases I tend to respond with, "Oh, you're fine," or some variation thereof. Here are a few handy alternatives:

Have a glass of water.

Sit down and rub it.

Read a book.

Walk it off.

Think about other things.

Did you brush your teeth today?

Lacking anything as trite as scientific fact to back me up, I believe the human immune system thrives best with a little neglect. Of course, this approach can be seriously flawed. One

could, for example, see one's daughter run headlong into a bas-
ketball pole while playing dodgeball. One could check her
daughter's vision, note she's speaking clearly, and, in fact, seems
eager to get back into the scrum. One could let her play for another hour, bring her home, feed her dinner, let her fall asleep,
and, while checking on the blanket situation an hour later, discover she'd thrown up in her sleep. Only then would one realize
she'd let her concussed child fall asleep unmonitored. For
months afterward, one could make oneself all gray and shaky at
the mere thought of putting her precious and only daughter to
sleep with a swollen, potentially bruised brain.

Thank God I never did that.

But this morning's complaint wasn't a matter of a skull and a
hard place. This was Alice learning what every woman who's
ever thrown herself into a bikini knows: sit-ups have teeth. After
every class, we could look forward to thirty-six hours of intermittent grumbling. She learned the word "abs" and threw it
around freely. Her abs hurt when she got out of bed. Her abs
hurt when she pulled off her sweater. Her abs hurt when she
sneezed. Her abs hurt when she coughed. Her abs hurt when she
folded laundry. Her abs hurt when she sneezed again. My response to all these statements was "Huh," which I thought neatly
conveyed, "I have heard your voice saying something," without
adding, "and I wish to hear a great deal more on this subject."

When she mentioned that her abs hurt when she put on her
seat belt, I finally realized I had to act, or be prepared to have
raised a person who, when grown, calls several friends to complain about how painful it is to detangle her hair.

"Sweetheart," I said, catching her eye in the rearview mirror, "I am going to ask you something and I need you to be hon-

est. Is the pain worse than it was this morning when you told me that it hurt to tie your shoes?"

[I asked because a friend's nephew complained about pain in his collarbone for a week and it turned out to be a symptom of leukemia. I can almost live with having let a child with a concussion fall asleep; I'm not sure I could survive being "the mother who ignored the first signs of liver cancer."]

She thought and said, "No, it's about the same."

I followed up with, "And it's the same pain you had last week, which eventually improved?"

Pleased that I finally wanted to discuss her discomfort in depth, she gave this some time. Finally, she said, "Yes, it's exactly the same pain."

"Then," I said briskly, "it's time for some bad news."

She leaned forward, fascinated and a little fearful. There was a small possibility this bad news could lead to an injection. On the other hand, she was the star of the story, and that never grows old.

"I am your mother," I continued. "Your very existence is fascinating to me. I will listen with interest to the small details of your life longer than anyone else in this world, including Daddy and the pets. Having said all that, I have no interest in hearing about your aching abs any more. Sit-ups make your stomach hurt. They make *my* stomach hurt. They make *everyone's* stomach hurt. This isn't news. From now on, you are given free rein to complain if something is truly painful. If something is only uncomfortable, or if you have complained about it before, you must do it in an entertaining fashion."

"What does that mean?" she inquired from the backseat.

"Amuse me. Complain in a way that makes me laugh."

"I can do that," Alice said, rising to the challenge.

"Oh, but I'm going to make it harder. You can't use the same complaint twice. If you want to keep complaining, you're going to have to find new ways to amuse me every time."

"Oh."

There was silence. The radio tried to lure me into buying cost-competitive rims. I mused over whether this mother-daughter conversation would at some future time pay for a therapist to redo her entire house, or merely the kitchen. I considered whether Alice might someday end up in the emergency room dying of a burst appendix because she couldn't think of a witty and entertaining way to describe four days of stabbing abdominal pain.

She spoke up again.

"Do they make small notebooks? Small enough for me to put in my pocket?"

"I can find you one. Why?" I asked, wondering whether this was a non sequitur.

"If I'm not home, or if I'm feeling okay but I think up a good complaint, I'll want to keep it for later."

I hope Alice's future therapist enjoys the chateau I'll buy her.

Modern Love

THIS IS HOW WE MATE HERE IN LOS ANGELES:

Day One. Meet at Motorola/Halo 4/Tampax promotional party. Within ninety minutes you have taken naked pictures of each other with your cell phone, which you promptly lose. Get engaged seventeen hours later. Celebrate your togetherness by being interviewed by *OK! Magazine* and retaining an attorney to sue the online gossip columnist publishing the naked photos.

Day Two. Break up. Send out a publicity release.

Day Two. Get back together. Send out a publicity release.

Day Five. Break up. Send out a copy of Day Two's publicity release.

Day Six. Get married in Vegas. Honeymoon in Disneyland, which you rent for your exclusive use. Imply to *In Touch* that you and your new husband used the spinning teacups in ways never intended by the original designers. Refer to each other as your best friend, your soul mate, your ideal lover, and the finest actor you know. Compliment him in print for his performance in *Crash*. Apologize in print for confusing him with Ryan Phillipe, whom you dated but no longer speak to.

Day Eight. Buy three ocicats. Name them Lola, Tallulah, and River, which, you tell *Us Weekly*, is what you will also name your three Chinese daughters, whose adoption paperwork you just started. Create a production company together. Call it ELF, short for Eternal Love Films. Buy seven books to make into movies, all of which will star the two of you.

Day Twenty-six. Tell *Parade* that marriage is hard work but that you and your husband are prepared to ride out the rough spots. Muse aloud about writing a book about the secrets to a long and happy marriage. When asked where your husband is, think a moment and then say "Arizona? No, the other A state . . . Alabama. I think he said something about getting barbecue. Or he's touring with his band. He's in a band, right?"

Day Twenty-eight. The *National Enquirer* prints pictures of you in a compromising position with your car detailer. *People* reports that your husband's new costar—a sixteen-year-old Korean-Austrian model—is flashing an engagement ring from your husband. Remove yourself from the city to lick your wounds. Realize that when you are outside of the city licking your wounds no one is looking at you. Come back to Los Angeles and alert the paparazzi that you plan to lick your wounds in solitude in the Coffee Bean & Tea Leaf at the corner of Robertson and Beverly.

Day Thirty. 10:00 a.m. "We are saddened to announce that we have decided to formally separate. We remain committed to each other and we ask that you please respect our privacy and the safety of our cats at this time."

Day Thirty. 10:05 a.m. Alert soon-to-be ex-husband by text message that you are divorcing him.

Day Thirty. 10:30 a.m. Send anonymous e-mail to gossip blogger who posted naked pictures, clarifying that soon-to-be ex-husband has a new strain of herpes and needs a body double for any movie requiring a shot of his naked butt.

Day Thirty. 11:00 a.m. Get served with papers from soon-to-be ex-husband because he is suing you for support and alimony for the ocicats, whom he renamed Adolph, Gotti, and Darth.

Sharp Left Turn

WHEN YOU LIVE IN LOS ANGELES, YOU KNOW TWO THINGS about your friends: (1) They have written a script and (2) they'd like you to read this script and give them constructive criticism.

You can avoid the phone calls, you can move several times and arrange to spend a few months in a medically induced coma, but when you wake up they'll be in your hospital room, smiling shyly and offering up a sheaf of battered pages. The title will be something soul-sucking like *Lenin and Marilyn: A Rock Opera*.

I have been known to read these scripts. I have been known to have tea with the writer afterward and to give notes, for all the good that does. The one lesson I've learned is that a writer asking for comments on his script really, down deep, only wants one comment:

"It's perfection!"

Or, maybe: "Don't change a thing!"

Or else: "I am retiring three vowels from my vocabulary, in honor of what you have achieved in this script!"

The writer is less enchanted when I take a long sip of my tea, and then another, and then I ask him if he wants a scone, and then I go to the bathroom and then I come back. Then I take another long sip of my tea, and then I check my voice mail. Eventually, having exhausted all available delay tactics, I inform the writer, "You have second-act issues."

To oversimplify, most movie scripts go like this: in Act One you introduce the people and present the problem; in Act Two you flesh out the problem; in Act Three you fix the problem, or don't—depending on whether it's a comedy or a tragedy. But many newer writers continue to add ornate emotional side trips and allegorical detours well into the second act when we should be zooming down the main plot highway. A new script will find us at the cusp of the climactic gun battle when it occurs to the writer, "Wouldn't it just rock if it turns out our hero was a hemophiliac? And he gets a paper cut during this big battle and he starts bleeding like crazy and his driver—wait, ooh! His driver who used to be his girlfriend but had plastic surgery and a sex change so he doesn't recognize her and came back for revenge for leaving her in jail but has fallen in love with him again—anyway, that character, whatever he or she is, has to take him to the hospital for a transfusion, where the driver suffers kidney failure, and then I can write all that stuff in about how I feel about socialized medicine . . ."

That is a second-act issue. If you are a highly talented and seasoned writer, you can thumb your nose at the whole structure business and drop in new plot twists anytime you like, but the scripts I read are not usually written by seasoned professionals. I mean, come on, *I'm* reading them. As for advancing your screenwriting career, giving your script to me is only one step more helpful than giving it to your toaster. These scripts are being written by hopeful amateurs. They are motivated by the endless possibilities of the blank page and their own fertile imaginations. I try to explain that the best stories, the ones that touch an audience for years to come, tend to have one shared characteristic: they are remarkably simple. Create a problem, flesh out the problem, and then solve the problem. If the first story you're creating makes you think of another story, then write a second story, separate from the first. Keep it simple.

Of course, what I don't tell these people is that I have a genetic second-act handicap. There's no narrative so straightforward that I cannot find a digression or a rant to lead me astray. Whenever I open my mouth that Microsoft paperclip leaps up with a bubble spelling out, "I see you are about to relate an anecdote. Would you like some pointless asides?" I always think *No! A thousand times no!* but within seconds I am fleshing out a story about picking up dry cleaning by tracing the lineage of the Bourbon family in Spain, which becomes a musing on crudités, which somehow steers me to the requirements for membership to the Junior League. I'd worry that my listener is confused, but they've usually slipped out of the room by then.

I am now going to tell a story about my prom night. Fully aware of my own second-act problems, I will indicate all such digressions with brackets.

I attended the prom with my friend Justin, because I asked him. I don't know why I cared about prom. I had no interest in the traditional teenage rituals. I was marking time in school until I could stop this hideous charade of being like people my age and go back to work. I cared because John Hughes and *Seventeen* magazine told me prom mattered in ways I couldn't begin to appreciate until I had actually been to prom.

Prom, it seemed, was kind of like Europe.

[No straight man I know cared even one-tenth as much about prom as the girls did, except for how they hoped to have sex afterward. Some of my gay friends had the potential to care about prom on an aesthetic level, but they knew they weren't getting their own special version of the dance in the fabulously decorated gym with the cutest guy in school. So they either went with a female friend or stayed home and watched MTV feeling lonely but also oddly hopeful for their college years.]

Justin could have taken one of the several girls who each labored under the delusion she was his girlfriend.

[They were all named Kimberly. They all aspired to one day appear in a ZZ Top video.]

Owing to some combination of mutual affection and the fact that I asked him five months before the actual dance, Justin and I went together. The prom was at a hotel down by the beach, in Marina Del Rey.

[Marina Del Rey was incorporated in 1965. Its last architectural detail was added about five years later. Marina Del Rey is all about faux-wood paneling and big square apartment buildings looming over small round pools, which long to be embellished with swinging Swedish stewardesses. I defy you to drive through Marina Del Rey and not start humming the theme to *Three's Company*.]

Corsaged and groomed, we headed toward the hotel where the prom was being held and promptly got lost. We both forgot to bring an invitation, and every hotel in the area could be described as "the large grayish-beige building with lots of windows, sort of overlooking the marina, with a sign advertising the all-you-can-drink Sunday brunch."

[All hotels, apartment buildings, and condominiums anywhere near the beach in Los Angeles have names with the word "Vista," "Mar," or "Pacifica" in them. This is so the guests know they are entitled to a view of the Pacific Ocean even if their actual view is of the air-conditioning unit at the Vista Mar Pacifica

Hotel next door. It also lets people know they are staying in a city that used to belong to Mexico.]

Just as we spotted the right hotel, a car lurched in front of us and stopped suddenly in the middle of the lane. Justin swerved to avoid hitting it and we slammed into a tree. We were doing thirty miles an hour. Neither of us was wearing a seat belt, but because I wasn't occupied with the immediate challenge of avoiding a collision, I had the extra millisecond to duck.

[We were in Justin's father's car. It was a Cadillac—the style and vintage where the bench seat not only had enough room for me to duck but, had I chosen, enough room to make a cassoulet.]

The car stopped moving. I sat up a few seconds later. The trunk of the tree we'd hit was about two feet from the windshield. The front third of our car was embracing the tree in such a way that both headlights now faced each other. The car we avoided hitting was still sitting frozen in the wrong lane, its owner staring at us blankly. I got out of the car and wobbled over on my high heels. Snapping into sudden wakefulness, the driver put his car into gear and raced off down the road away from me. I was now quite certain this jerk was seriously drunk. I was also quite certain he was the evil toad who just ruined my evening so I raced down the street after him yelling, "STOP!" like maybe he had just *accidentally* sped away and my squeaky-voiced rage would bring him to his senses. Between my heels, my hairdo, and my dress, I wasn't anyone's idea of a serious threat.

[Oh, the dress. Remember, this was the early 1980s. I longed for a hot-pink strapless taffeta number with a poofy skirt. My mother, showing an Olympian restraint, never said, "Quinn, at your height and weight, you'll resemble a toilet-paper cozy." She merely suggested simpler lines and classic colors. I sneered. But one lucky day, while browsing through an antiques store, she found *the* dress. It was from the first decades of the twentieth century, lacy, ankle-length, and narrow, a poem of simple lines and classic colors. It fit me perfectly. It was also filthy. It cost forty-five dollars to buy and another ninety to be laundered by someone who could be trusted with antique lace. It came back a warm creamy white. It was distinctive and elegant, and for the weeks leading up to prom I kept going into my closet—where it lay in a special linen bag—just to gaze at it. It was elegant and flattering but it was not the ideal outfit for a quarter-mile dash after a drunk in a speeding car.]

The drunk screeched around a corner, and I stomped back toward Justin's car. A few people were now milling around. Someone said he called the police and got the license plate on the other car. This very kind stranger gave me his phone number and told me to have the insurance company contact him if there was any problem.

[Days later, I called the phone number, to thank him.

"Pentagon," the voice answered.

"Wrong number," I apologized and hung up. I dialed again.

"Pentagon."

In a dubious voice, I asked for John D—. I was immediately connected to another office.

"General D—'s office."

It turned out that our Good Samaritan was a brigadier general in charge of all overseas communications for the U.S. Army. Whatever my feelings about the military-industrial complex might have been, this was a seriously cool witness to have on our side.]

I returned to the car and plopped back in the passenger seat. Considering my options, I decided to have a good mad-cry. Justin, who had been leaning against the steering wheel, turned to face me and said, "I'm sorry Quinn, are you okay?"

The streetlights on the lesser avenues of Marina Del Rey provide just enough light to see when one's date appears to be bleeding from several gashes in the middle of his face. Justin turned his head toward me, causing his blood to splatter in a wide arc across the front of my dress. In order to keep the proper tone, I responded to him in an upbeat voice while staring at his earlobe.

"Oh," I said waving a hand airily, "I'm fine. *Fine.*"

He passed a hand over his face and looked wonderingly at his palm.

"Did I cut myself?" he asked.

I glanced at his face for an instant and went back to staring at his earlobe.

"Oh. You have a . . . little cut," I said brightly. "We should probably get you to a doctor. You know, just for the heck of it."

[I'm going to brag here. I'm kind of fabulous in an emergency situation. The same energy level that, in day-to-day situations, makes people want to hit me over the head with a pipe flattens out to normal when I get an adrenaline blast to the brain. Also, when someone as moody and pessimistic as I am finds herself in a crisis, I become almost jovial. *Look,* I think, *the worst thing—which I kept predicting would happen—has happened!* Worriers like me enjoy having our suspicions confirmed.]

Justin leaned his head against my shoulder. The kind witness stuck his head in the window and told us the ambulance was on its way.

Justin said, "What happened?"

I said, "We hit a tree."

Justin said, "My dad's going to kill me."

I said, "I doubt it. It wasn't your fault."

Justin said, "I'm not going to be pretty anymore."

I said, dryly, "Even now, you're still prettier than I am."

[He always was. Had I been as pretty in high school as he was I would never have needed to develop a sense of humor.]

[Justin swears he didn't say that. He did.]

I watched his blood drip into my lap. Then he said, "What happened?"

We did that a few more times as we listened to the ambulance drive in circles trying to find us.

[Fun fact: The streets of Marina Del Rey were patterned after the doodles of a middle-school girl in double-period algebra.]

The blinding lights inside the ambulance shooed away any fantasy that all Justin needed was a Kleenex and a cab and we'd be on our way. His initial diagnosis was a fractured nose and facial contusions. He went into the bowels of the ER to be sewn up, and I wandered into the waiting room where I sat alone watching *Knight Rider* without sound. I noticed what appeared to be clots on my skirt. My hands started to shake.

Needing something to do, I decided to call my mother. Searching for the pay phone in the corridor, I planned out everything I would say. I would calmly explain about the accident, I would assure her that I was unharmed, and explain that I'd get a ride home with Justin's father. I located the phone and used one of the quarters she had given me for whenever I needed to make an emergency call.

"Hello?" she said.

Sob, sob, sob, sob. Sniffle. Deep inhale. Sob, sob, sob. Deep inhale. Attempt to explain this isn't the world's weirdest obscene phone call. More sobbing. More deep inhales. Sob some more. Sob some more. Sob some more.

Apparently, the only thing sustaining my composure since the collision had been the absence of my mother's voice. I promised to call her as soon as his dad arrived but insisted on staying to support Justin.

[Because I was such a source of calm and reason at that moment.]

[By this time I was now a snot-sodden, tear-stained, blood-clot-bedazzled mess. It's humbling to realize that even with a fractured nose, at that moment Justin was still prettier than I was.]

I hung up the phone and sobbed a few more minutes. Eventually, I headed back to the ER, but because I was still sobbing, I got completely lost. This meant that prior to finding my way back to the ER I visited nearly every area of the hospital, including the radiology wing and the morgue.

[I still wonder what the patients in the Cardiac ICU thought as they opened their morphine-dulled eyes and saw a sobbing, white-cheeked figure in a blood-spattered Edwardian dress drifting through their room.]

By the time I found the waiting room, Justin's father was there. Looking down at my hands, I noticed I had been holding something. I didn't remember picking them up nor did I feel them in my hands for the last hour, but there they were, sticky and bloody. I handed Justin's dad the keys to what was left of his car.

Justin emerged, his blackened nose and eyes contrasting nicely with the waterfall of dried blood down the front of his shirt. He hugged his father, then he put his arm around my waist and hugged me. Shoulder to shoulder, our heads leaning toward one another, it was the prom picture we'd never take.

Weeks later, Justin and I took off for pancakes during a free period. Tossing my backpack in his backseat, I noticed a familiar-looking clump on the floor. Gingerly, I lifted up his blood-soaked shirt and the tuxedo jacket. I held out the shirt and waved it around like a flag taken from an especially grim battle. Justin said, "Oh, there they are."

"You're supposed to return this," I explained.

"Yeah," he snickered. "So I can get my deposit back?"

A flake of dried blood sprinkled down onto the upholstery. I crammed the clothes back under the rear seat and thought about my beautiful dress. It had been sent to a particular dry cleaner, one I can only imagine specialized in the laundry needs of butchers and ax murderers. One hundred and fifty dollars later, it was unmarked by the evening. If you looked at the dress, it was almost as if the evening had never happened.

Our evening had taken an abrupt turn into a tree and ended up someplace I had never anticipated. It wasn't cute and it didn't move the story of my life forward; it was just a random event. Had this been in a script, I would have said wearily to the writer, "Yeah, that got my attention, but what's the point?" And the writer might say, "It's like life."

And I'd sigh, take a sip of tea, and say, "True. But sometimes life could use a rewrite."

The Spirit of '76

PEOPLE CLOSE TO ME HAVE BEEN GIVEN ORDERS. WHEN I finally die of good intentions, I don't care what is sung at my funeral. My only feeling about flower arrangements is that I suspect I will hate carnations even beyond the grave. There is, however, one point on which I must stand firm: I must be buried in a striped shirt, jeans, and Converse low riders. It's not that I think this is my best look; I'm just concerned that mourners might not recognize me in anything else.

I used to try to look stylish. From the early 1980s through the mid-1990s, I was never fully out of the fashion pool, even when it was abundantly clear I hadn't waited twenty minutes since eating and was at risk of a style cramp. During this time, there was no look so high-concept I didn't try to recreate it on a budget—which, in my case, was like creating a do-it-yourself poodle by gluing together clumps of dryer lint.

In high school, I owned bronze ballet flats. Realizing a sizable part of my dignity was only feigning death in the corner, I also bought a matching bronze headband, which I wore, a la Olivia Newton-John, about an inch above my eyebrows. No one ever confused me with an Australian singing sensation, but several people did point out my resemblance to the piccolo player in the *Spirit of '76* painting. A few concerned friends asked if I'd been in a car accident. "Yes," I wanted to shout. "A fashionable car accident!" But we trendsetters let our head bandages speak for themselves.

I saved up several weeks' allowance to buy a pair of forest-green, velveteen corduroy knickers. Having studied every issue of *Seventeen*, I knew that these knickers—when combined with an Aran sweater, white tights, and black patent-leather flats— would give me the appearance of an English country girl, all rose-cheeked and flush with love for my horse and that tousle-haired boy on the next estate who would marry me and make me the Duchess of Rutland. Sadly, there were a few ruts in my road to an inherited title. For one, I lived in Los Angeles, a place where titles are never inherited, but negotiated. The local temperature rarely drops below sixty-five degrees, so I didn't own an Aran sweater. I decided a short-sleeved white angora sweater would provide much the same effect, and having blown my entire allowance on the green knickers, my bronze shoes would have to stand in for the black patent-leather flats. Also, there was the problem that I don't flush winsomely. Really, I don't flush at all. Where others develop pink cheeks after a brisk workout, I just become a more uniform shade of gray. The son of the Duke of Rutland, upon seeing me dismounting a horse, would assume I had been shot. The bronze head bandage probably wouldn't help.

But I'm nothing if not willful, so I soldiered to school in my new outfit. With the bronze and the angora, the overall look was less English countryside and more Israeli discotheque. As the thermometer approached eighty-five, bits of angora came loose and stuck to my lip gloss and gray sweaty cheeks so that I soon resembled Santa Claus at an Israeli discotheque. The headband was removed for surreptitious blotting of the armpits and back. Colin, the best-looking boy in our class, walked up and stared at me for a full thirty seconds. Had I been capable, I would have blushed. He finally said, "You know what you look like?"

Hardly daring to say, "An English girl in the country who just got off her horse?" I instead said breathlessly, "What?"

He thought a second longer and said, "H.R. Pufnstuf."

No, that was impossible. Pufnstuf had green legs and white boots. I had—I looked down—green legs and white tights. I didn't have a bowl-cut hairdo of orange polystyrene, I had a . . . longish bob with bangs. Oh, Lord, I did look like H.R. Pufnstuf. I longed to snap back, "Pufnstuf wished he had bronze ballet slippers," but something told me I needed to reclaim my self-respect, not set fire to it.

Never again have I tried to wear knickers, plus-fours, culottes, or gauchos in public. This proves I have learned exactly one thing in my life. But every other ill-advised fashion choice? Oh baby, watch me go.

Watch my shoulder pads for about three years there in the mid-1980s. Please. Watch them. They were supposed to attach to my bra straps to shift visual focus upward but they had a bad habit of sliding down the back of my shirt, creating more of a dowager's hump thing. This provided the same effect of distracting the eye from my hips as the more conventional shoulder-placement would have, but it also led to worried questions about my calcium intake.

Watch me in the late 1980s wearing a black catsuit, platform shoes, and dangly earrings. What I hoped made the statement "1950s Sarah Lawrence artsy-yet-exotic dance student," was actually read as "Jimmy Dean ninja sausage roll." The same outfit led to a memorable adventure where I managed to hook my earrings through my matching bracelet, purse strap, and hairbrush at the same time. This took five people and twenty minutes to untangle. It would have taken less time and fewer people had all my housemates not been completely stoned. Something about my situation struck them as unbearably funny and caused them to crave maple sausage during the entire rescue, further complicating matters.

Observe me during the grunge cycle in my Dr. Martens and loose-fitting calf-length jumper dress. Please note my resemblance not to the girlfriend of the lead singer of the band, but rather to the girlfriend of the lead singer of the band's Okie grandmother—back when she fled the dust storms in the 1930s. I would look in the mirror and think, *I appear to have huge feet, thick ankles, a baby on the way, and a husband whom I share with four sister-wives back on the compound. I wonder why I don't date more often.*

Contemplate the one time I thought, *Why do I keep wearing black to formal events? I should try color.* Please note how the color, which was a lovely bright tangerine in the store, became traffic-cone orange in evening light. People kept shading their eyes to look at me. I eventually draped myself in my date's jacket, claiming to be cold, just to avoid scorching people's retinas. This led to the second dumbest formalwear-based concept I've ever considered: "Color is problematic, but patterns are fun." Unfortunately, the pattern in question exactly matched the wallpaper in the reception room. Look carefully at pictures from that event and you can see a spectral blur. That was my arm, which I kept waving so the caterers would stop leaning folded tables against me.

Scrutinize the pink tweed suit I bought after seeing it shown so well in *Vogue*. Sadly, it didn't occur to me that the reason the models look so winning and adorable in this look, besides being a foot taller than I am and having the best tools Photoshop could throw at them, is that they are typically fifteen. Post-pubescent girls in matronly outfits can look sweetly incongruous. A woman well into her thirties in a pink tweed suit looks sixty. When I wore it, women tended to curtsy when I walked past. Men offered to find me a chair. Many people already enrolled in AARP called me "ma'am."

Every two years I convince myself a well-chosen scarf will save me from my own dismal fashion sense. I buy one and play with it for an hour until I notice I'm obsessing over poofiness. If the scarf poofs in front, it says to the world, "Hi! I'm eating lobster!" If the poof is on the side, it says, "Bet you don't see that coffee stain on my shoulder now, do you?" If the poof is in back, it cries out, "I'm so proud of my Girl Scout troop!" At which point I decide enough things are shouting at me in my life already, so I tuck the new scarf in the drawer along with the many other casualties of my periodic need to accessorize.

I once bought a sexy and expensive sweater-dress, not realizing that my dress had been born a wide knit belt and—much like the eels compelled by some inner GPS to travel thousands of miles to breed in the same sea in which they were born—it was time to return home. Nothing makes a holiday party more festive than death-gripping each side of your dress so it will stop trying to shrink its way up to the old country. All pictures of me from that event could be subtitled "Quinn fights with her dress and grimaces in terror at the thought of the sit-down portion of the evening. Merry Christmas!'"

And yet, I still love fashion. I love fashion magazines when they tell me with a straight face that I would be well served by yellow eye shadow and should buy it right away and—wow! what are the odds?—there is an ad for Yves Saint Laurent yellow eye shadow on the very next page. I love stylists and photo editors who make choices that probably only make sense to people who have dined exclusively on antidepressants and small bits of beef for the past ten years. Here's this season's hot cover model in a hat made of roofing shingles and Play-Doh. *Yes!* Here's a tableau of diamond-encrusted watches in what's obviously the photographer's colonoscopy. *Marvelous!* Here's a montage of ten-thousand-dollar purses being worn by anorexic teen models dressed as homeless people, lying on beds of crab cakes. *Brilliant!* It's all so flagrantly stupid and fascinated by itself that I cannot help but find it adorable.

Because I read this nonsense constantly I have inadvertently developed some knowledge of how things are done this year. Combine this with having a mother who impressed upon me that clothing actually looks better when it, you know, fits, and my own dogged need to be of service to humanity, and I become a nightmare in a clothing store. Pray you are not in the dressing room next to me, for you will get my opinion.

I was standing in the dressing room at J.Crew recently and feeling the mild disappointment that is my typical emotion in a dressing room. After all these years I am still convinced there is a pair of pants somewhere that will make me appear five feet ten and of Swedish ancestry. There was a knock at the dressing room door.

"How are those pants working out?"

"Right size but the wrong color. Could you possibly get me this style in the khaki?"

There was a puzzled silence.

"They don't come in khaki."

"I saw them on the same table, in khaki."

"I'm sorry, but they don't come in khaki. We have walking shorts in khaki, would you like to see those?"

"Just clarifying here. The front table, right as you walk in, has three pairs of pants."

"Yes."

"One was gray, one was olive, and one was khaki. I am currently wearing the olive, and I would like the khaki, please."

I could hear her brow unfurrowing through the door.

"Oh, *those*! Sure, I'll get them. But those aren't khaki, they're birch," she explained, her voice fading into the store. Silly me. I waited in the dressing room, refolding sweaters and listening to an exchange between two young women in the next dressing stall.

GIRL 1: That's so cute on you!

GIRL 2: You don't think it's too tight across the stomach?

GIRL 1: No!

GIRL 1: Doesn't it seem to be bagging in the chest a . . . lot?

GIRL 2: No! And the pants are adorable!

GIRL 1: I think they might be too tight. Look, they're pulling across the hips and the butt, and I can't actually button them.

GIRL 2: Are you kidding? You look great!

I was hooked. Apparently, these two people were looking into different mirrors. Under the pretense of finding out whether my not-khaki-but-birch pants were en route, I quickly put on my clothes and walked into the public dressing area.

The woman trying on clothes was modestly endowed; she had a bit of a tummy and a rear end that was large without being shapely. The camisole top drooped lifelessly over her chest but clung to her abdomen like a poultice. The fitted pants weren't just pulling across her hips and butt, they were struggling at every seam. The bell-bottom legs widened at the knee and revealed more than a few inches of too solid ankle flesh. In short, this woman was not well served by this outfit, nor was this outfit well served by her.

Her friend cooed, "You know what would go great with that? A fitted jacket. And an ankle bracelet."

This was such a preposterous statement that I took a careful look at the speaker. She was a marvel of female design, curvy and skinny, lush and toned. She was also wearing a camisole top and fitted pants, their perfect fit making a mockery of the outfit currently insulting her companion.

"Maybe . . ." the larger woman said slowly, plucking dubiously at the camisole straps, "if I got them shortened, it would fit better. And got the bra cups taken in. And had the bottom loosened a little bit."

This is the point where the voice in my head, Lady Helpful, started yammering. "*Say something,*" she insisted, poking my brain with her index finger. "*No, please,*" I whined. "*She won't listen to me and they'll both think I'm weird. Besides, who takes the fashion advice of someone wearing* these *shoes?*" I looked down at my Converse low riders. Once cream, they were now a faded beige accented with a spattering of poster paint, half a My Little Pony sticker, and a few splotches from a cat's bout with intestinal flu.

Lady Helpful glowered. I glowered back. *"Look,"* I argued with myself. *"What's the worst thing that happens if she buys the outfit? She looks vulgar and a little fatter than she actually is. Have you been out in the mall? This isn't a problem anymore."*

I had reached a standoff with myself. But then, as usual, I caved. I took a deep breath and cleared my throat to get the girl's attention.

"Uh," I began. "You know, camisole tops like that are cut on the bias. It might take more work and money to tailor than it's worth. And there's another cut of pants that have a straighter leg." Saying this allowed my mouth to move without letting out what I was really thinking: You are a big, beautiful woman who needs to stick your fingers in your ears and hum loudly when your skinny, delusional friend gives you advice about what to wear.

They both glanced at me, and I felt my face turn bright red. Mercifully, my khakis—I mean, my birches—arrived, which gave me a reason to slide back into my dressing room. As I closed the door there was a conspiratorial giggle from the next room.

"Glad I could entertain them," I said to myself. *"Wasn't that humiliating for me. And she's still going to buy ill-fitting pants."*

"Yes, but I was right," Lady Helpful said airily. *"And my being right felt good. And since I live in your head, your external mortification means nothing to me. Now, put your striped shirt and jeans back on, lace up your Converse low riders, and buy me*

a cup of tea or I'm going to tell the woman we saw by the three-way mirror that the blouse she was trying on makes her look like she has tertiary syphilis."

I wanted to ask this voice where she was when H.R. Pufn-stuf was stalking in the wings, but I decided I'd had enough of her for one day.

Carson Has Two Mommies

ALICE AND I WERE DRIVING SOMEWHERE. WE HAD JUST LEFT karate class and the last time I had looked in the rearview mirror she was trying to loosen the knot on her day-glo obi. My mind drifted. Did I just think we had string cheese at home or did we actually *have* string cheese? Was Alice going to demand string cheese once we got home? Should I get string cheese at the nearest store? Was string cheese reason enough to battle Gelson's parking lot on a Saturday afternoon—a cruel tarmac where mothers armed with Expeditions and BlackBerries play chicken with each other while popping *The Princess Diaries* into the backseat DVD player?

Alice announced, "Carson has two mommies."

Carson was a cherub-faced, redheaded boy in karate class. Being six, Alice rarely noticed any adult attached to any of her peers unless the adult was offering up Cheetos or a kitten. Today, however, both of Carson's adoring and attentive mothers were *en dojo*, one cheering him from the sidelines while the other nursed his infant brother behind the trophy rack. Either activity might have been what caught Alice's attention, prompting her to count parents and consider their gender. I waited to see if she'd add anything, but she didn't. She was waiting for me.

"Yes," I finally said in a voice that wanted to be flat but came out cautious. "Carson has two mommies." I had hoped my tone would finish the conversation but I had just played the overture.

"How?" she shot back.

I briefly flirted with "They found him in a cabbage patch at an Indigo Girls concert," but decided my daughter was ready for a few basic facts of life in the big city. First, however, I needed to issue a stern warning—a binding nondisclosure clause, as Consort would say—so my kid wouldn't start giving PowerPoint lectures to her peers whose parents were hoping for a few more months of innocence. I caught her eye in the rearview mirror.

"I will explain how they did it," I said in my best parental voice. "But if I find out you've been passing this information along to your friends, the consequences will be horrible. Do you hear me?" She nodded her head quickly and tried not to squeal.

Without preamble, I explained: (1) egg, (2) sperm, and (3) fetus. There is something to be said for introducing the birds and the bees from the perspective of two women trying to create a child. With two mommies, you don't have to go into the specifics of how sperm actually gets from the generous male friend to the lesbian with the egg. As far as Alice knew, FedEx might be involved. Having covered a fairly loaded subject quickly, accurately, and vaguely, I let out a sigh.

After a moment, Alice said, "So that's how all families with two mommies get babies?"

And I said, "Yes . . . *mostly*."

"What do you mean, *mostly*? What other ways are there?"

Couldn't shut my mouth could I? Couldn't just leave it at "yes" and go back to ruminating about string cheese? Of course not. Because a fussy part of my brain thinks things like, *You can't just give her* half *the information. Not all babies in lesbian families arrive through an ice chest and a turkey baster. If you only tell your child part of the facts she will be underinformed. Or worse, misinformed. If you don't tell her the whole story, she'll end up getting her artificial-insemination facts from the gutter.*

So I did what any modern parent would do. "Oh, *look*! A Chihuahua!"

But she stayed on message. I slumped. "Keeping in mind this isn't to be discussed outside this family?" I stalled.

"I know. Just you and Daddy."

Frankly, I didn't see Consort carving out special time for this conversation either. I mentally scanned her inventory of friends.

"All right, Ivy has two mommies. But one of Ivy's mommies was married to a man before she fell in love with Ivy's other mom. So Ivy has a dad, not just a . . ."

I froze. I couldn't think of a child-friendly version of the phrase "sperm donor." Luckily, Alice was already on to another thing.

"So Zack's mom got sperm?"

"Which Zack?"

"The one who eats his hair."

"Always wears shorts?"

"Yeah."

"No, his mom adopted him."

The subject was dropped as abruptly as it came up. Alice grabbed a book and I switched on the radio, confident I was in the clear. The clear, however, was short-lived because Alice's consciousness had been raised and over the next few days it dawned on her: *my friends all got here somehow.* Because we live in Los Angeles in the bloom of the twenty-first century, the pathways to life are rarely straightforward.

"Adam doesn't look like his parents."

"Yes, Adam was born in Tajikistan and his mom and dad went there and got him."

"Where is that?"

(Silence)

"Um, Eastern Europe."

[Stupid 1970s educational system, worrying about our self-esteem but completely doing away with geography. Alice never asks me questions about how I *feel* about myself.]

"Was his sister born there?"

"No, his sister was born in Peru."

"Were Emily and her brother born in Tajik . . . Tasik . . . that place?"

"Emily's fathers found a very nice lady who would give them an egg and use their sperm to make a baby. And then, two years later, another baby."

[Actually, I believed there was a second lady who gave them an egg, on top of the uterus lady, but when my brain bubbled up to clarify this detail for my daughter, I slapped it silly and forced it to shut up.]

"Merrit told me she grew in her aunt's uterus."

"WHAT DID I SAY ABOUT MENTIONING THIS AT SCHOOL?"

"I didn't! She tells everyone that. All the time."

A casual call to her mother the next day confirmed that yes, Merrit had been the product of her mother's egg and her father's sperm but owing to medical complications had come to term by way of her aunt. I also confirmed that Merrit found this tidbit so fascinating that—no matter how much her mother might beg her otherwise—she led with it, conversationally.

I can only hope Alice honored her nondisclosure agreement on the playground, but the variables continued to fascinate her. We were at the library a week later when she spied a mother and child in line; she whispered at a volume heard all the way to the books-on-tape-and-homeless-guys area, "Mommy, look! That Chinese lady adopted her baby from China!"

Under the guise of searching for something in my purse, I hissed in her ear, "Or maybe that's her biological child." This puzzled her, so I whispered a short, discreet, yet scientifically accurate version of the more conventional route to parenthood. By that point, we were in the checkout line. This might not have been the ideal venue for starting the basic birds and the bees canon, but the woman ahead of us was disputing a ten-cent late fee, so we had plenty of time.

Alice thought about this new method of procreation for a few moments, then shook her head. This was way too easy. Where were the surrogate uterus, the multiple sires, the court system? In the modern age, a child in a big city knows fewer and fewer parents who just got knocked up. What used to take a bottle of Chianti and the back of a VW bus now involves a team of fertility specialists, a second mortgage, and/or the goodwill of the Chinese government. Alice, a child who appreciates a lively pageant as much as the next kid, clearly preferred twenty-first-century breeding.

A few weeks passed and my daughter stopped discussing the ways human families are created. I assumed we were out from under the awkward question spotlight. In fact, I was feeling quite pleased with myself. I had covered a large and ungainly topic calmly and thoroughly yet without once resorting to terms commonly found in Penthouse Forum. Let other parents fret over how to navigate this perilous journey with their children. I had it nailed.

One night a month or so later, while driving home from the beach, a small voice issued from the darkness of the backseat: "What happens when we die?"

At that moment I experienced a glorious epiphany. A sudden realization, like a blinding flash of white light, hit me from above. I now understood that *all* of the major life conversations between my daughter and me were going to happen in a left-hand turn lane.

I stalled. I coughed. And as I did, I remembered that when Alice had been a mere infant, I had waffled long and hard on the whole Santa thing. It's terribly sweet to watch them put out cookies and write notes of innocent desire, but the more you play up the myth, the more likely you are to find a slightly older child pondering practical considerations such as, "How could he possibly visit every house in one night?" and "I never did get a reasonable answer as to how he gets into houses without chimneys" and "Why didn't the security alarm go off?" At some point the child figures out she was lied to and, even if it was in a loving and well-meaning way, it's a lie from parent to child. I couldn't get comfortable with that. Enough people in this world are going to lie to her; I want her to know her parents are one place where she gets the truth. On the other hand, denying Santa from the get-go just seemed churlish.

So, when Alice was a little over a year old, I had an inspiration. She had noticed Santa in a book for the first time and inquired about this bearded man in the strange track suit.

I began, "That is Santa Claus. *It is said* that he lives at the North Pole."

Did you catch that? With a simple addition of three words—"it is said"—I could live with myself. Alice had the entire story and could choose to believe it or not. I was neither espousing nor denying the existence of Santa, I was merely passing along some interesting information I'd heard. Were there a court case involving old Sinter Klaus, I could not be called to testify, as my information was, at best, hearsay.

I also kept the holiday focus off the big guy. If Alice's childhood could be thought of as a sitcom, Santa had a very small cameo. He wasn't the wacky neighbor, popping in weekly with his catch phrase, his crazy hairdo, and the second-act complication. No, he was more like the affable bar owner who has a couple of good lines each season. At Christmas, he never gave her the big present and I never used him as a form of behavior modification. Of course, this limited my discipline arsenal somewhat, but it also assured me I'd never see Alice make finger quotations around the word "Santa" as in: "If *Santa* has a problem with my unmade bed, maybe *Santa* should just talk to me himself."

Turns out, the heavy-artillery topics of birth and death aren't that far removed from the whole Santa thing. I waffled between what I knew, what I wanted her to know, my instinct to tell her the truth, my cellular-level impulse to keep her away from unpleasant truths, and an unrelated but pressing need to complete a left turn in busy traffic.

I stopped coughing and started talking. I told her that while no one knows what happens after you die, I believed we left our bodies when they were worn out but that our souls continued.

"Where?" she interrupted.

"Um, somewhere."

"Tajikistan?"

"Probably not."

But somewhere. Then, to keep the afterlife relevant to her, I threw in my belief that when you die you get all your old pets back. Having been called upon to describe the unknowable with less than a minute's warning, I sat back in my seat, spent but satisfied. I had earned another maternal merit badge today, of this I was certain.

"You said, you believe that's what happens," said the prosecuting attorney in the backseat. "Don't you know?"

"As I said," I repeated, slightly deflated that no one but me seemed impressed by my handiwork, but still driven to *not lie* to my kid, "no one knows. People believe. Some believe very deeply, but we don't have scientific evidence of what happens after death. In order to prove it, we'd have to have what is known as empirical evidence . . ."

Suddenly, anguished wails drowned out my lecture on scientific method.

"WE'RE ALL GOING TO DIE AND YOU DON'T KNOW WHAT'S GOING TO HAPPEN AFTER I DIE AND I'M GOING TO BE ALONE!"

Didn't I handle that well? For those keeping score at home: Telling the nearly whole truth about reproduction worked. Not expressly lying about Santa was maybe a bit devious but it allowed me to sleep at night. Allowing room for reasonable doubt about the afterlife forced me to pull over on the Pacific Coast Highway and comfort my hysterical child for half an hour.

While birth took a little over a month to stop being front and center in her mind-share inventory, death took half a year. And this meditation did not follow a measured pace. We'd be going through our lives, enjoying the simple pleasures of a day in the park, a slice of pizza, or the second act of *The Nutcracker*, when out of the blue Alice's face would crumble and she'd moan, "We're all going to die, and we don't know what happens. I'm so alone!" I speak from experience when I say that very few eighty-dollar ticket holders appreciate a sobbing six-year-old existentialist and her tongue-tied mother during the Dance of the Sugar Plum Fairy.

Tentatively, I began to ask other mothers for insight, and I soon learned that every child went through his or her wrestling match with mortality. From wanting to disinter long-dead hamsters, to inquiring of elderly relatives when they planned to breathe their last, to insisting on sleeping with Baby Jesus from the crèche, every child I knew went through a death fixation of some sort. And all of them got over it.

The good news was that my ham-handed approach hadn't broken my child. The humbling news was that being honest with her probably hadn't changed anything either. The children of the devoutly religious people I spoke to struggled with the shadow of death as did the children of atheists. I could have told Alice that when our bodies stop working the angel Fred Astaire shows up with a gigantic bag of candy corn and escorts us to the Barbie Valhalla in the clouds, and we still would have gone through this.

It dazzles and humbles me that I am supposed to give advice on such big topics. I still don't understand how string cheese peels. Because I love Alice so very much I try to forget that I'm an idiot. I try to give her words to live by. I want her to make every effort to live with courage, confidence, an awareness of other people, and an abiding humility in her own powerlessness. That's what I want to tell her. What comes out, as we buckle in for the ride home, is that life is like a left-hand turn in busy traffic. If you're careful and lucky, you'll do okay.

Poetry in Motion

SOMETIMES WHEN CONSORT AND I ARE FEELING AFFEC-
tionate, we debate which of us will die first. Being as I am female
and he is male, I'm quite certain he is going to die first. Actuarial tables and a visit to any retirement home would support my
theory. Sometimes I find an actual actuarial table online. I print
it out and wave it in front of him, basking in my rightness. He
will die first. I will cry and cry and cry and then I'll get his side
of the bed.

Whenever he is informed of his mortal inevitability, Consort
always shakes his head and says, "Yes Quinn, if you were a *normal* female you'd outlive me. But you're *you*."

Then, to drive his point home, he brings up some violent
and unlikely injury I have suffered. He will mention the time I
was riding a horse and dismounted so I could lead us safely
across a stream and proceeded to walk the horse across my foot,
breaking my toe. Or the time I was running up a flight of stairs
to a fencing lesson and I stumbled and landed on my own foil,
removing a chunk of shin bone in the process. Or the time I
developed blood poisoning from a spider bite. Or the time I got
pneumonia and coughed so hard that I broke a rib. It's a poi-
gnant fact of my life that whenever I visit the ER, I provide a
nice change of pace for the medical staff beyond the usual stab-
bings, heart attacks, and the drunks with the d.t.'s.

What's hard for people treating these injuries to imagine is that I'm always as surprised as they are. I'll be walking along, it's a lovely day to be dropping off library books, and a second later I'm removing a chunk of tequila-soaked glass from my forehead. This is the basis of Consort's argument. It's not that I lead a life devoted to extreme sports and high-risk behavior. It's that my very cells call out to the sharp, the flammable, the suddenly preciptious, and the easily riled. When Consort confronts me with such anecdotes, I parry with a waved hand and an airy "Things like that don't happen to me anymore. I'll outlive you and then I'll crack my neck in whatever room I want and you'll just have to listen to it in the afterlife and suffer." Then I crack my neck. End of discussion.

Recently, I awoke in the middle of the night to the sound of our dog acting up. Generally, Rupert is a quiet, mellow dog, but his ruckus was urgent enough to rouse me from a sound sleep. Assuming he needed to go out, I staggered to the back door only to be confronted with Consort coming back in from the yard, the dog at his side. They both looked pleased with themselves. I muttered, "Is he okay?"

"Oh, yeah, he's fine," Consort answered, breezily. "It was tree raccoons."

It's a testimony to my ability to leave a warm bed, walk the length of a house, and make small talk without actually waking up that I nodded in agreement and went back to sleep. The next day, I called him at work.

"I'm sorry, tree raccoons?"

Yes, tree raccoons. The night before, sometime after 2:30, Rupert had grown suddenly very excited about the subject of *out*. He had to be *out* now. Out is the new black. *Out! Out!* Consort, being annoyingly nocturnal, was still at his desk working.

He was about to let Rupert out when he realized the sudden excitement might be over a skunk, a skunk who might not relish a new canine friend lunging forth to play sniff-my-butt. Consort locked the dog in the house—which caused the barking mayhem that woke me up—and headed outside to shoo away whatever it was spooking the dog. He saw no skunk, but he did see a cat waddling around the far corner of the yard. It was a huge cat. A very huge cat of indeterminate origin.

Consort went back in the house, got a flashlight, and determined that the monster cat was, in fact, a monster raccoon. It trundled over to the biggest tree in the yard and scampered up with surprising grace—Consort later described it as being like watching Chris Farley rock climb. Tracking the raccoon in the beam of his flashlight, he discovered no fewer than four more raccoons up in the tree, all of Samsonite heft, lounging about on various limbs, staring down with a menacing indifference. For reasons that I'm sure made sense when normal people would have been sleeping, Consort decided to shoo them away. He made a whistling noise; they continued to stare. He shouted like a cattle driver; they blinked. He poked at the tree with a rake; they yawned and opened another bag of Funyuns. Eventually, Consort determined that waving the bamboo rake back and forth like a giant fan made a noise they found displeasing; or else their pity for him was cutting into their appetite. Either way, they tumbled down to the high stucco wall next to the tree and ambled off into the night.

I was fascinated. Tree raccoons! I guess it made sense that raccoons would be up in trees—at least until they saved enough for the down payment on a condo—but I had never actually considered finding raccoons in my trees. I made Consort swear that if he ever spotted tree raccoons again he'd wake me, even if I swung at him with my patented fist-of-sleep while he tried. Consort, confused that someone in the house was even more excited about tree raccoons than the dog, agreed warily.

The very next night, as I was gearing down for bed, I went to the back door to let in the cat. Typically, Lulabelle is ambiguous about her return to domesticity, at least until last call, at which point she comes flying toward the door as if Cerberus, Hades's gatekeeper, were breathing down her neck. Then she freezes inches from the threshold and spends a few minutes dithering about whether she really wants to come in or not. I remind her that Indoors = Kitty Stars by shaking her bowl. She shoots me a filthy look for thinking she can be bought that easily and saunters into the laundry room. Then, in one powerful leap, she finds the bowl on the dryer and attacks her supper. It's all wondrously predictable. On this night, however, I called for Her Grace several times without getting an answer. I looked out into the shadows of the yard but saw no football-sized fur missile careening toward the door. Instead, in the glow from the porch light, I caught a glimpse of two eyes shining down from the tree.

I squinted. Raccoon or cat? Whatever it was, it was stealthy and coy. I stepped a little farther out into the yard, but the dark shape didn't emerge clearly as either a cat or a raccoon. If it was a raccoon, I wanted to see it. If it was my cat, I wanted to shout at it, however impotently, to come inside. I returned to the house, found a small flashlight, and walked back toward the tree, standing directly underneath it. Whatever it was, its body was hidden behind a branch. I took a step sideways; still hidden. Another step sideways; still hidden. Another step sideways and my foot hooked under the wooden Adirondack lounge chair, one of only two objects in the entire backyard. The momentum of catching my foot caused me to arc sideways over the chaise, the leg of the footrest now helixed with my leg. I landed on the ground, and a second later the heavy teak frame landed on top of me. A half-second later the flashlight hit me as well, right on the face.

I lay on the ground, staring at the night sky, or what I could see of it through the top half of the tangled chaise that was pinning my head to the ground. Through the slats, I saw the animal look down at me. It was, I was disappointed to note, Lulabelle. She appeared to be thoroughly disgusted and embarrassed for me in equal measure. Sighing, I righted the chaise and carefully folded up my pant leg to avoid bleeding on yet another piece of clothing. As I'd done many times before, I mentally calculated my tetanus-shot status and was happy to note I was unlikely to develop lockjaw. Then I went inside to tell Consort he had my permission to date after I was gone.

The Good Soap

IMAGINE YOU ARE IN MY HOUSE SOME EARLY EVENING. DINNER has been eaten. Consort is indulging in his favorite leisure sport: squinting at something on the computer screen, tapping a few keys, swearing, and squinting again. Alice is at the kitchen table indulging in her favorite leisure sport: not doing her homework. This is the half-hour of doodling and humming that has to occur before fifteen minutes of homework is accomplished. Somewhere, quietly, the cat is hacking up a hairball and the dog is shedding. I walk into my bathroom, at which point our domestic peace is disturbed by a pained and insistent shriek that reverberates from every wall in the house.

"Who fondled my good soap?"

I don't know which is more pathetic: that my life has become so small that I've grown jealous and protective of a bar of soap or that no one else in the house takes my soap seriously. I certainly give it the respect it deserves. It lives in a little paper bag inside a little cardboard box, which has absorbed some of the soap's fragrance and gives off the intoxicating scent of roses, geraniums, and leisure time, perceptible even to a woman whose nose might as well be constructed out of cement.

If Consort and Alice are to be out of the house for several hours, I will go to its sacred hiding place and liberate the good soap. Holding it lovingly in my hands, I will take it to the bathtub, place it carefully in a slotted soap holder, and then I will draw a bath. While soaking in this bath, I will read a book. This book won't always be about the British royal family, but it will frequently be about the British royal family. When I am not adrift in the calming sea of British royal history or turning the increasingly damp pages thereof, I will lather up a healthy dose of my good soap. Much later, when I am relaxed, wrinkled, scrubbed, and scented, I will emerge from the tub. I will carefully dry off the good soap in a clean washcloth, slide it into its paper sleeping bag, and tuck it into its little box. I might even pat it fondly before I hide it away again. Let no one think I take my good soap for granted.

Alice was with me when I purchased the good soap. It was a glorious pink, the color of the cheeks of healthy babies and wealthy spinsters. I held it to Alice's nose and she scowled. "You know I don't like roses," she said.

I smiled silkily and murmured, "Good, because it's not for you. It's mine. My soap. For me. Not for Daddy. Not for you. Not for trimming a beard or becoming a life raft for My Little Pony. It's just for me."

"I don't want it anyway," she sniffed.

"And you can't have it," I shot back.

"Fine," she said.

"Fine," I said.

Having settled that the soap was (a) not hers and (b) mine, I bought it. I took it home and placed it in a drawer in the bathroom. An hour or so later, I came in to wash my hands. My new soap was sitting in the bottom of the sink, wet and sudsy. I yelled, "AL-ICE!" and waited for her, while watching several drops of expensive soapy goo slither down the drain. Alice wandered in. I pointed sharply into the sink.

"My good soap is in the sink. Why is my new soap in the sink?" I sputtered, carefully picking it up and blotting it dry. Alice stared off into space, thinking. She thought the entire time it took me to search for and locate the engraved paper sleeve behind the small trash pail under the towel rack. It was crumpled but recoverable.

"I needed to wash my hands," she finally answered.

I breathed in, I breathed out. I tried for a reasonable tone. "Remember," I said in a conspicuously well-modulated voice, "how this was *my* soap and *not* yours? Perhaps I didn't make myself clear. Please don't use it." I slipped the soap, now carefully dried, back into its sleeve and into its perfect little box, which I found in the tub, filled with Barbie shoes.

She thought for a second longer and hit upon a flaw in my reasoning. "You're the one who always says I have to use soap!" she said triumphantly. I felt the blood drain from my head all the way down to the earth's core the way it does during certain mother-daughter conversations.

"Yes, I do demand you use soap. But there was soap here," I said in a slightly strangled tone, pointing to the large and cheap bar of white waxy crap sitting dry and unloved on the sink ledge. "And here," I said, pointing to the bottle of fluorescent-green liquid with Dora the Explorer and her simian friend splashed on the front (because when I think *clean* I naturally think *monkey*—an animal known for flinging its own poop).

She tilted her head toward the other forms of soap and considered them a moment. "Oh," she finally said. "I didn't see those."

Because that's my child's vision, her world-view. The thing directly in front of her cannot be seen. It is completely invisible unless pointed out by a parent with a raised voice. But the thing that is deep in a drawer behind the backup Q-Tips and a manicure kit is agonizingly apparent. I held up the good soap and spoke slowly in my lowest register.

"This is my good soap. Don't use it."

Alice nodded. I felt nodding wasn't enough. I pressed on.

"I'm not kidding. If you use my soap, you will have to pay for another out of your allowance."

She slumped her shoulders and sighed again. "O-*kay*," she said finally and shuffled back toward her room. I tucked the good soap back into the farthest depths of the bathroom cabinet, confident we had communicated and ever hopeful that, at some point in her childhood, we'd get through an entire conversation without one of us sighing.

Two days later, I went to take a shower. There in the shower caddy was my good soap, a steady drip from the showerhead gradually boring a hole through it. The soap was at least 20 percent smaller than it had been the last time I saw it. This caused me the odd sensation of feeling my own blood pressure without the little balloon-y thing. Consort had been the last person to take a shower, and Consort views any water left in our thousand-gallon hot water heater as a damning testimony to his not having tried hard enough. I followed the scent—my scent—of roses and geraniums into our bedroom where a half-dressed man was deciding on a tie. He picked up one tie with a greenish-brown pattern, held it to his neck, and asked, "What do you think? This one? Or . . ."—he held up another tie with an identical greenish-brown pattern—"this one?"

"The first one," I said confidently, knowing he'd spend another ten minutes on the decision before selecting a yet-unseen third tie with a greenish-brown pattern. "But," I continued, "that's not why I came in. You used my good soap."

He looked puzzled. "I did?"

"Yeah."

"Why did I do that?"

"I don't know."

He thought and I waited, because I don't have hobbies.

"Oh, I know," he said with some relief. "It was because I couldn't find any other soap in the bathroom."

Scientists will be excited to learn this affliction is genetic. I gently blotted what was left of my soap and tucked it into its bag and back into its box. Then I stood in the bathroom and tried to think like the two of them. It was predator and prey and I was going to win this round. I couldn't leave the soap anywhere in the bathroom because it seemed that leaving it anywhere near running water was the same as saying, "Could you two please make some rose-and-geranium-scented drain paste?" I had a flash of inspiration. My lingerie drawer! It would stay hidden and dry while also scenting my unmentionables. Oh, that's good, that's the kind of thing French women do. For months to come, I would give off an olfactory note from the underwire, which would hint oh so subtly at my feminine wiles.

I fairly skipped into the bedroom, opened the drawer, and was flummoxed by the sight of Alice's socks. Then I remembered: her antique dresser was showing its age and her sock drawer had recently taken to flying off its runners and attacking the fingers of any small girl trying to find tights. So until Consort fixed the runner we were sharing a drawer. My feminine wiles would be bunking with Shrek anklets. Alice would come looking for themed footwear but she'd leave with an expensive bath toy. No good. I looked around the bedroom. The closet? Oh, nice. I could hide the soap in one of my dress pumps, which don't get worn unless someone is getting married or buried. Everyone I knew seemed healthy but also fearful of long-term commitments. These shoes weren't going anywhere anytime soon.

I hacked my way toward the back of the closet and looked where my dress pumps usually lived, next to my *I'll get back to riding when I have free time and discretionary income, which probably means after Alice gets through graduate school* paddock boots and my *I don't care how much my feet bleed, I paid full retail for these and I will wear them again* evening heels. The dress pumps weren't there. A quick-yet-thorough tearing apart of the house found them nestling in the loving bed of a marabou stole in Alice's dress-up box. It seemed the shoes only got worn for marrying, burying, or a practical-yet-witty counterpoint to a gypsy costume.

Brushing aside a *Ranger Rick* magazine and a cutaway Great Pyramid made from shirt cardboard and gold-painted Pez, I sat on the couch and thought. Even a first-year psychology student would have suspected there was a larger problem here than soap. The problem was the total lack of boundaries I had created for myself. Without my noticing it, my daughter and my life partner had invaded every private place in my life and then peed in the corners. I did a thorough inventory to determine the degree of infestation.

My purse carried a pair of Consort's glasses, two Polly Pocket dolls, Consort's backup cell phone, a book of Mad Libs, and a Barbie cowboy hat. It also carried my wallet, which contained ten redemption tickets won at a Chuck E. Cheese three years ago, but no cash. My car contained a combustion engine, several air bags, a bunch of knobs and dials, and the answer to the question: I wonder how many books about princesses and/ or cats were published last year?

With Alice, the boundaries are just so very blurry, which makes sense in a biological way. I remember hearing about a study that explained how fetal cells from a mammal's offspring could drift around within the mother's bloodstream for the rest of her life. This only confirmed what I suspected: I will never be totally alone again. The first dwelling Alice ever experienced was me. When she was no larger than a baseball, she made me drive twenty miles for freshly made tortillas. We've been hashing out who owns what ever since.

She eats off my plate. I lick my thumb and clean her cheek while she howls. I don't wear bangs because Alice can't stand bangs and I can't stand hearing about how she can't stand bangs. She wears bright colors because she's the closest I'll ever get to turquoise. Asking her to view the soap as *not ours* but *mine* was as bizarre to her as insisting the soap wasn't subject to the laws of gravity. We'd eventually get to soap autonomy, but only after years of behavior modification. In the meantime, I took to stowing the good soap in my purse, which meant Alice only found it when rummaging for a mint or a pencil or her blue leotard.

One night, very late, my eyes snapped open and my head sprang from the pillow. Silhouetted in the bedroom door was Alice. Having arrived well into the first act of this particular episode, I struggled to fill in the details. It was night. Alice must have said, "Mommy?" My maternal alert system would have sprung into action, which puts me in a totally wakeful state without actually switching on my higher brain functions.

"What is it?" I asked, trying to remember her name. "A nightmare?"

"The blanket came off," she said, shaking her head, "and I couldn't sleep."

Ah, there's the brain coming online. I could feel it whirring away in there, getting up to speed, spitting out such questions as, *And it seemed easier to walk all the way down the hallway than pull up the blanket at your ankles . . . ?* and *When it's seventy degrees in the house, how much did you need that blanket, anyway?*

But what she was really saying was, "I have a powerful need to rejoin my pack."

Our communal cells vibrated happily at one another. I wiggled over a bit and patted the pillow. Even in the near darkness, Alice saw the invitation and leapt nimbly into bed. Within a minute, she was asleep. I knew she was asleep because she started expanding.

Alice offered her usual "Thank you" for being allowed into our bed; she lengthened her arms and legs by up to a yard in each direction. Interestingly enough, this new length was mostly comprised of elbows and knees.

Consort, on the other side, had a more subtle approach. When we first moved in together, I offered him whichever side of the bed he wanted, and he chose. He swears he has never reconsidered his decision, but each night, once asleep, he longs for my side of the bed and he will achieve it, one patient inch at a time. Given eight hours, Consort will claim the entire bed to himself, leaving me a sliver of territory down by the footboard, at which point Lulabelle will leap nimbly onto the bed and start inflating to the size and density of a keg of beer. Between Consort, the kid, and the cat, I was a modest nation with no natural borders staving off constant sorties from aggressive superpowers. I had become Poland.

The annual father-daughter trip to play in the snow brought a welcome respite from this relentless personal invasion. I stood in the doorway, waving good-bye lovingly and, it must be admitted, more than a bit enthusiastically. Three days! Three glorious days where I didn't have to model good habits for anyone. I could eat carbohydrates for every meal. I'd eat pie with ice cream and watch daytime television and have a bath with the good soap whenever I felt like it. In fact, I'd have a bath right away. I brought out my new book about the Hanoverians.

The bath was lovely. So was the brunch of pecan pie, the afternoon snack of pecan pie, and the early dinner of pecan pie and house-renovation shows on TLC—my version of dinner theater. Consort called. He and Alice had arrived at snow and were happy. I was happy and I was happy that they were happy. But since I had developed what I diagnosed as a "crust headache," I went to bed early. I sprawled with glorious abandon. I tested out Consort's side of the bed. I stretched across the bed. I tried lying on the diagonal. No one got in my way. Even the cat was sleeping elsewhere tonight. I was free.

I was also wide awake. Since the last time they had gone out of town, I had forgotten how to sleep without someone trying to steal my pillow. The bed felt less like open space to be claimed by me than empty space I wasn't capable of filling up. This is what life would be like without them, I thought, which made me get up and head into Alice's room. I curled up in her bed, her stuffed animals weighing down my feet. The cat jumped on the bed and wedged herself into the small of my back and immediately began agitating for me to move. Something hard pressed into my cheek from under the pillow. I pulled it out and flipped on the bedside light; it was the good soap box. I placed it back under the pillow, its soft aroma mingled with my daughter's unmistakable pillow perfume, and fell soundly asleep.

Through the Great Room, Past the Gym

THIS HOUSE, THE HOUSE IN WHICH WE LIVE, IS NOT LARGE. There is enough room for all the living things—two adults, the one child, the dog, and the cat—but it was built during a time when people were shorter, had less stuff, and were pretty excited by a roof not made of hay.

When I bought this house, I was the only one living in it. I am not very large. The house is not very large. This worked. At its best, when the house wasn't collapsing or leaking, I appreciated how it was scaled down for me, like my own domestic Disneyland. When you're five foot three, twenty-foot ceilings just remind you that you're paying for square footage only the flies are enjoying. Then Consort moved in and the house contracted slightly. He was off-scale to the house and it punished him by creating extra corners at just about shin height for him to discover. We were starting to think maybe we needed to find a larger place, one that didn't resent him personally, when Alice arrived and the house went back to being the right size. She was so very small, and I wanted to be no more than a few feet from her at any time, so the house, obligingly, made itself into a cozy nest. I was never more than an arm's reach from a cloth diaper or a fresh change of clothing for either of us.

About this time, we went to visit a business associate of Consort's at his mini estate in a fashionable neighborhood. His wife, a ferociously educated and meticulously groomed woman, gave me the tour of the house, which she had helped design. I was dazzled by the size of it, easily ten times the area of our house, but I was puzzled when she gestured down one long hallway and said, "That's the girls' wing." I peered down the elegantly appointed tunnel toward where I guessed her eight-year-old twin daughters' rooms were and asked, "And your bedroom is *where* again?"

She laughed an educated and groomed laugh and pointed the other way. "Through the great room, past the gym." I glanced down at my tiny daughter, asleep in her stroller, and couldn't imagine designing a house that would put me that far away from her. Must be an older-kid thing, I figured.

As it turned out, the kids weren't the only ones in that family with distant beds. The husband had a whole second family in another country. The divorce was as sordid as the house had been icily pristine, spare and spacious and perfectly designed to keep every member of the family a stranger to each other.

As Alice grew we kept planning to move, but every time we'd start thinking about it, housing prices would climb to a new and more ludicrous plateau. Around the time Alice turned two, I overheard what someone paid for a bungalow down the block and realized with a jolt that we could no longer afford to move into our own house. The fact remained, there was something sane about the house we had now: the size of it; the environmental footprint; the monthly nut. We stopped talking about the move and started talking about the renovation.

However, talking about renovating is not actually renovating; we have yet to get around to the renovation. At first, the renovation didn't start because Consort is a perfectionist and I get bored easily. He would bring home seventy-eight different tiles so we could pick out the ideal kitchen backsplash, and after the third tile I would use my trick of sleeping with my eyes open. Then the renovation didn't happen because we had to choose between the perfect kitchen or keeping Alice in extracurricular activities. If she didn't have extracurricular activities, Alice would never get tired, and there is no backsplash in the world that makes up for a child who is not tired and will not go to bed and wants to watch *The Daily Show* with you.

We lived in a small house. We continue to live in a small house. Alice does not live on the other side of the great room because there isn't one room in this house that could be defined in size or quality as being "great." If my child calls for me in the night, she doesn't need to use the phone. We are, for better or worse, a family that knows one another. When a family lives in as close proximity as we do, the first thing to go is privacy. How can I keep forgetting to lock the door when I enter the bathroom? More intriguing, perhaps, is what kind of powerful pheromones do I emit when I enter the bathroom, and why must every living creature be drawn to them? I walk in and shut the door. After the perfect amount of time to get myself into an embarrassing state, the door bursts open and Daughter strolls in.

"Hi!" she announces, cheerily.

"What did I say about knocking before coming into the bathroom?"

Alice tries to remember, and decides whatever I said was superfluous, so she answers with, "I want Mexican food for dinner."

"Well, this isn't a restaurant, you always want Mexican food for dinner, and it's nine thirty in the morning. Did we really need to discuss this now?"

We stare at each other. Then she remembers something vital to her health.

"I cut my leg. I need a Band-Aid."

"Where?"

"In the medicine cabinet."

"No. Where did you cut your leg?"

Alice cannot find said injury to her leg.

"No, wait. It's on my hand."

"Alice, please go find your father and talk to him and leave me alone."

She leaves. After a beat, there is a knock. "Person in here!" I bark.

"I know," Consort answers through the door, somewhat perplexed. "Alice said you wanted to talk to me?"

"No, I want *you* to talk to *her*. I want *you* and *me* to have some romance left in our relationship, so can I please have some time to myself?"

"Of course. Of course."

Out in the hallway, I can hear Consort retreat and Alice approach.

"What did Mommy want?"

"She wants some alone time, honey. Let's take the dog for a walk."

"I don't want to."

I could have told him that. Alice, athletic as she is, is growing up in Los Angeles and views her feet as something to be adorned, not used. The dog, having heard the word "walk," comes prancing excitedly to join Consort and Alice in the hallway. The dog needs his nails trimmed, so now, along with the sounds of my family negotiating a walk, are the sounds of a touring company of *42nd Street* rehearsing a big number right outside the bathroom door.

"Put on some shoes, sweetie, and we'll go out for a nice walk."

Alice sighs and, sensing the inevitability of being forced to use her feet, tries to make the whole experience at least visually pleasant. "Can I wear my new shoes?"

Simultaneously, from two different sides of the door, Consort says, "Sure, whatever." And I shout, "Not the new shoes!"

Alice stands closer to the door and negotiates.

"Pleeease?"

"No."

"PLEEEEEEEEEEEASE!?!?!?!"

"Absolutely not. Those are your new dress shoes."

The door slams open again. Alice and dog enter as one. The dog places his head on my knee and looks up adoringly. Consort stands just beyond the threshold, looking apologetic. The cat slips through the open door and starts batting around a disposable razor.

Alice begins pleading, "I want to wear my new shoes!"

Seeing no hope of ever being alone, I offer a compromise. "How about cowboy boots?"

"Fine," Alice snorts, after a sulking beat.

Consort tries to hustle everyone out, but Alice stands her ground.

"Now what?" I demand.

"I have to go to the bathroom," she explains. "You all have to leave."

.   .   .

When you live in a small house with a child, you can't get away from the child as easily as big-house owners can. There is no gift-wrapping suite or maid's yoga-room where I can banish my offspring should I feel so inclined. There is only her room, and eventually I will have to go in there, if for no other reason than half my winter clothing is stored in her closet. In a small house, the kid is always around. For the most part, this pleases me. I rather enjoy looking at and talking to my kid. Still, I lose all composure when it comes to being the governess of good habits. I blame this on proportion.

In a large house, the bed of a child, lavishly unmade, might represent less than 1 percent of the entire domestic acreage. In our house, if Alice throws off the blankets just right, I will be stepping over them on the way to and from the garage. Dishes left on the kitchen table comprise less of a big home's overall visual composition than the hand towels in the downstairs guest's second bathroom. In the more modestly sized home like ours, you can see the dishes on the table from almost any point in the house, just as you can see the Eiffel Tower from almost any point in Paris. In the small house, every design choice takes up a larger proportion of the visual space. That's what I mean by "proportion." Were we to move into Hearst Castle, wet towels on a bathroom floor wouldn't even register on my housekeeping radar. In our house, a wet towel either needs to be picked up immediately or risks being designated as sculpture by a city inspector.

Another aspect of snug living means none of us will ever say, "Gosh, how long have you had that unconscious habit?" We know exactly how long you've had it. We even remember how good life was before you had it.

Consort hums a single line of a song, over and over. He doesn't hum the whole song because that would give it closure. He doesn't sing it, which might draw his attention to the fact that he's doing it and cause him to stop. No, he gets some unimaginable subconscious joy humming the same line over and over. Forever. Or until I start to claw at my skull.

He'll be in the office, cleaning out e-mail. I am in the living room, mere feet away, reading a book. He is humming the first line to "Can the Circle Be Unbroken," an upbeat little number about someone burying his mother.

CONSORT (Humming): I was standing by the window . . .

Consort breathes. I wait. He clears out another e-mail.

CONSORT (Humming) I was standing by the window . . .
QUINN: Honey?
CONSORT: Hmm?
QUINN: Humming.
CONSORT: Oh, sorry.

Consort breathes, clears his throat.
Reads another e-mail, deletes it.

CONSORT (Humming): I was standing by the window . . .

Forty-five minutes and ninety standing-by-the-windows later, I finally sing at the top of my lungs "ON ONE COLD AND CLOUDY DAY!!!!" Consort jumps about six inches off his seat.

CONSORT: What the hell was that?

QUINN: The second line of "Can the Circle Be Unbroken."
    You kept singing the first line.
CONSORT: I did? I don't think I even know that song.
QUINN: I can assure you, you know one line.
CONSORT: Sorry, I didn't notice.

Consort turns back to the e-mail. I open my book. A blissful moment of silence occurs. I read my book's first line for the seventieth time.

CONSORT (Humming): The moment I wake up, before I
    put on my makeup . . .

Of course, our little Alice is test-driving her own unconscious habits, which I won't go into here because on her they're adorable and I think she inherited most of them from me anyway. Still, I think she's pleased to note how virtually all of them make her mother fly from the immediate area and hide in the bathroom, where, as we know, no sanctuary can be found. Sometimes I hide in the garage and dream of a day when I can shout imperiously, "Alice, you go to the lesser playroom and you, Consort, stay in the music salon, and I don't want to see either of you until 6:30 tonight, when we'll meet in the light green dining room." But the reality is that I'd go looking for them within an hour; the magazine-reading room would be too lonely without them.

Consort, Alice, and I were curled up on the couch watching a documentary about meerkats. We watched them dart down into their underground dens, curl up with their family members, and groom each other with loving care and surgical precision. The narrator told us how meerkats, after days spent in the hostile desert, thrived in the closeness of the den.

I looked down. I was absentmindedly braiding Alice's hair as Lu slept in her lap. Somehow the cat continued sleeping as my daughter snapped Scrunchies on her tail. Alice's feet were propped on Consort's leg. Rupert, not allowed on the couch, was attempting a flanking invasion of Consort's lap with a move best described as "oozing upwards." Every member of the family was within inches of one another. I considered getting some pretzels but realized there weren't enough pretzels to bring back and share, nor was there a hidden place in the kitchen where I could jam a handful of food in my mouth. Instead, I leaned back against Consort and watched these exotic mammals gather strength and comfort from one another against the harsh world outside.

Al Dente

WHEN I WAS PREGNANT WITH ALICE, MY WISHES WERE SIM-
ple. A boy would be fine. A girl would be fine. He or she should
be a happy little person who didn't have my immune system or
my coloring. A girl arrived and fairly quickly it was established
that, unlike her mother, she did have a hope in hell of tanning.
This was good. Within a year it was determined that, again unlike
her mother, her immune system didn't take every cold germ as a
personal challenge to spawn lung disease. Again, good. Having
done so well on the first two wishes, I leaned close over my new
child and whispered, "Sweetheart, now try to get Daddy's teeth."

I was born with Wal-Mart-sized choppers in a bodega-sized
mouth. This led to all sorts of excitement as my adult teeth
erupted in places not traditionally thought of as chewing areas.
For the sake of future eating, I was rigged with a palate stretcher,
a plastic-and-metal apparatus that extended across the roof of
my mouth up behind my snaggly teeth. In the very top, in the
dark recesses of my palate, there was a lock—a lock that needed
to be turned a quarter turn every night, using a key of dollhouse
proportions. One of my earliest memories is of my mother hov-
ering over me, flashlight tucked in the crook of her neck, peer-
ing and poking into my gaping maw. "DO! NOT! MOVE!" she
commanded. "DO. NOT. SWALLOW."

There's really no card that conveys, "Thank you for widen-
ing my head, Mom."

You'd think something that medieval would be adequate to the task of straightening my teeth, but all it did was create enough room for the adult teeth to find their way into my mouth. It didn't make them any smarter. My teeth slid down sideways. My teeth leaned against one another like drunken frat boys. A couple of teeth, showing an embarrassing lack of initiative, came halfway down and stopped. I spent the next six years in one tooth-improving gizmo after another.

Because I was acting at the time, they couldn't just give me Big Iron and be done with it. Instead, they kept putting me into Half-Assed Plastic, which was one-quarter as effective and took three times as long—sort of like near beer. The logic was that metal braces were obvious and unattractive, while plastic braces were unnoticeable. I'll grant you, braces made of metal are noticeable but at least the human eye registers there is something on the teeth. With plastic braces, my teeth were simply out of focus, and what you saw of them had a shade of yellow that suggested I was the only sixth grader starting her day with three cups of coffee, a glass of red wine, and a Camel. Eventually, sometime before I was old enough to rent a car, the last retainer was lost, the last payment was made, and I was declared to be orthodontically sound.

Considering that my mother's teeth came in straight, as did my father's, it seems especially unfair that my parents had to go through such effort. Whichever ancestor foisted these dental genes upon me had the good sense to die before blame could be assigned. Now it was my turn and as each of Alice's teeth came in, I'd look at it and think, *Not sprouting from her nose. This is good.* Because that's what I'm all about: realistic expectations. Alice tanned, she didn't have a runny nose eight months every year, and her teeth were approximately where they should be. Maybe my more troublesome genetic material had been given a generational time-out.

When Alice was four, the dentist took her first X-rays, cleaned a little, poked around for a few minutes, and motioned me over. We stood by the dental chair while my daughter sat paralyzed with pleasure at the *Toy Story* video on the plasma screen above her head.

"Do you have dental insurance?" he asked.

"Yes?" I said hesitantly, hoping this was some sort of poll.

"Because Alice is going to need braces," he said.

I felt that was a little abrupt. If you are consigning me to years of monthly dental appointments and having to buy generic cheese it seems to me I should at least be taken into a private room and offered a box of Kleenex, a glass of water, and a package of flavored floss. When my future earnings are being pillaged, I don't want to hear Tim Allen's voice.

"But," I spluttered, "they're so nice and straight! These are good teeth!" I was about to explain how she couldn't possibly have my teeth because she could tan when he stopped me.

"Yes," he said, gently lifting Alice's lips to show me her choppers. "They're straight. They are also tightly packed. When these teeth fall out, there will be no room for the next teeth. They will come in up here," and he motioned to her gums, "and here," pointing to her cheekbones, "and maybe a few here," he said, indicating her forehead. Alice flapped away his hands, which were interfering with her television viewing. I plunged into despair. My dental shame was coming home to roost. My troublesome DNA slipped away from the time-out corner and did a dance of triumph in the middle of the room.

You don't just *get* braces for your child. You *earn* braces for your child by virtue of numerous appointments for plaster cast making, mold forming, and credit checking. By the time Alice and I arrived for the official presentation of the gear, I was humming "Pomp and Circumstance." We were brought into a small room with a model of Alice's jaw already wearing the apparatus. Alice, alert to any opportunity for self-improvement, agitated to put lipstick on her plaster doppelganger. This time, I was offered water by the hygienist. It came in a tiny cup with the cast of *High School Musical* grinning out at me in their perfect, gleaming teeth.

The appliance was presented. Alice was to wear a palate stretcher for eighteen months, which, over time, would create enough room for her adult teeth to grow in. I wouldn't have to attack her open mouth with a key every night, but we would have to haul across town every three weeks for a tune-up. This would comprise a ten-minute appointment with a forty-five-minute commute on either side. Years from now Alice will ask, "Mommy, what did you do about global warming?" and I'll be able to tell her, "I contributed."

This expansion process was referred to as Stage One. Math was never my gift but calling something Stage One implies there will be other, equally expensive and time-consuming stages to follow. My dental insurance caps orthodontic payments at fifteen hundred dollars, which we reached when Alice touched her first *Highlights* magazine. I toyed with not doing Stage One and just letting the Stage Two chips fall where they may, but by then Alice would be chewing with her eyelids and elbows. Holding the plaster model of her teeth in one hand, I signed the contracts with the other. The term "indentured" kept popping into my head.

For everyone involved, the palate stretcher represented new levels of commitment—financial, emotional, and logistical—and within weeks it became abundantly clear this was not the best time to bring new levels of responsibility into our lives. I was distracted and overbooked by life in general and Alice had reached a developmental stage that was driving me out of my mind. To her credit, at least she was giving me something new to find maddening. This wasn't the limit-testing of an earlier time, or the spike of sassiness that recurred every ten months or so. When the palate stretcher arrived, Alice was more than willing to work within the system, as long as the system rewarded her periodically with visits to Web sites that featured pictures of kittens. She was just vague. There was no request so small that I didn't need to spell out every single detail, and no part that was self-evident to Alice. If, six months before, I would have said:

"Please make your bed before we leave."

I was now saying:

"Please go into your room, where you sleep. Not our bedroom, where you sometimes sleep, but the room where your bed is. Please remove all stuffed animals from your bed. Please remove the cat from your bed. Do not dress the cat in your clothing. Put the cat on the ground. Stand up again. Flatten the sheet on the bottom, to remove wrinkles. Take the top sheet, the one that is in a pile at the bottom of the bed, and pull it up to your pillow, and flatten the sheet against the bed. If there is a lump under the sheets, press it. If it's soft, it's your stuffed animal; remove it. If it squeaks, it's your cat; remove it; put it on the ground and do not dress it in your clothes. If the lump is neither a stuffed animal nor the cat, flatten it out. Now, you will notice another pile at the bottom of the bed. This is your quilt. Please pull it up and straighten it. Straighten means the quilt is on the top of the bed. If it's covering half the bed and puddling on the ground, that isn't straightening the quilt, that is giving your mother the headache she gets behind her eye. Having straightened the quilt, please take all the stuffed animals and place them on your bed. Finally, you will notice a third pile at the foot of your bed. It is a nest of socks that need putting away. They needed putting away three weeks ago when I first mentioned them. They desired to be put away two weeks ago when we had a discussion very much like this one. Last week, they were practically begging to be put away. Either you match them and put them away, or I cut them into tiny squares, soak them in kerosene, and use them as fireplace starters. I will give you no new socks, and you will develop smelly feet and that's all anyone will remember of you from grade school."

To which Alice would hear:

"Put socks on the cat."

Until her brain came back online, we weren't good candidates for new, pricy, fragile, expensive, tiny, costly, custom-made dental objects. But if we waited until she could actually hear me, her palate-stretcher case would be sitting next to her estrogen-replacement pills. Every now and then, I'd think, *Forget the sweet and temporarily absent-minded child, I'll just be responsible for those expensive doohickeys that look exactly as if the orthodontist plays with paper clips while he's on the phone*, but there were two problems with that approach:

One, I'm supposed to be teaching Alice personal responsibility and accountability and all that stuff that takes far more energy than just doing their work for them.

Two, I can't handle constant, low-level responsibility any better than Alice can. At least she's going to grow out of it.

I'm great in a crisis and epically bad at maintenance. My feeling is that if I do something boring and virtuous, I should be rewarded by not having to do it again for many months. Doing your taxes, as grisly as it is, fits perfectly into my model. It's horrible, it takes over your life for a few days, and then it's gone again until next year. [If you are the sort of person who just thought, *But Quinn, if you did a little bit of your tax preparation every month of the year, you wouldn't have to live on chocolate-covered espresso beans for five days in April*, then fine. *You* come over and take responsibility for the palate stretcher.]

I can keep track of more details than NORAD. Alice's shoe size? Got it. Presents for the godsons for Christmas? In a bag behind the extra ironing-board cover in the laundry room. The cat gets the eye drops, the dog gets the ear drops. Don't walk outside at night in spring without making a lot of noise ahead of time unless you've always wondered what a skunk looks like up close and startled. Without prompting, I can sing "My Sharona" from start to finish. For fun—and because I was afraid people might think I was too hip—I do crossword puzzles, which means that every month or so I learn three new names of rivers in Belize. I know all of the names of Alice's stuffed animals, which is no small statement because their names change an average of once every eight days. I also know the names of all of Alice's classmates who, because we live in Los Angeles, are frequently named after rivers in Belize. At last count, the moist computer in my skull has over three thousand small programs up and running. There is simply no room left to take on two objects that weigh less than a butterfly and cost more than my first car.

I could try asking Consort to be the keeper of the dental gear, but his day is pretty full trying to find any one of his many pairs of eyeglasses. Consort has reading glasses, driving glasses, driving glasses that allow him to read maps, reading glasses that allow him to drive short distances, sports glasses, glasses that are scratched and worn but still good enough for cleaning the garage, and glasses that keep him from falling down while walking the dog but aren't clear enough to let him see what he is picking up in the plastic bag. A man driven to flailing despair because he can't find his picking-out-paint-chip glasses doesn't want to hear about a palate stretcher.

In the end, the kid and I were in this together, and I am both pleased and shocked to note it didn't go as badly as I might have predicted. She'd leave her night gear someplace bizarre, but I'd find it while trying to locate my keys. I'd start the lecture after finding her palate stretcher in the drying rack by the kitchen sink, and she'd point out that, in fact, I was holding *my* night guard, which keeps me from grinding my orthodontically straightened teeth into a fine powder. We have discovered a nice bakery near the orthodontist's office where, post-stretching, we get sustenance for the long journey home. I think we might actually make it through this adventure.

And someday, when my mental decline is complete and Alice has put me someplace soft, warm, and—if she's feeling generous—accredited, I will live for her visits. And I'll use my last bits of sentience to demand that she smile.

Dog Days

I WAS DRIVING ALICE TO SCHOOL WHEN I NOTICED A BROWN dog trotting down the sidewalk. The dog—even from a distance, an obviously sociable mutt—nosed a woman walking past and attempted to play with her dog, a taupe poodle in a plaid coat. With minimal effort, the woman and her poodle ignored the brown interloper who, sensing a cold shoulder, proceeded to sit back on her haunches and have a good scratch. This entire scene played out in a leafy residential neighborhood that borders a commercial boulevard near Alice's school. I glanced up and down the street but could see no one calling out for a wayward pet. The dog had no collar and her paws were filthy. She finished her ear scratch, gave the sidewalk a quick surveillance, and loped off toward the busy avenue. My stomach sank.

From the back seat, Alice said, "I don't think that dog has a person."

"I think you're right," I said.

I pulled over to the curb and got out. Realistically, if the dog was lost, it would be in a mild panic and wouldn't let me get anywhere near it. I was afraid it might bolt directly into the busy avenue and the outcome would be horrible.

I said softly, "Hey, sweetie, you lost?" I beckoned with I-know-the-good-scratching-places fingers.

The dog grinned widely. She dropped down on dog elbows and crawled, soldier style, to me. She rolled on her back and licked my toes. Ten minutes later, Alice and I drove up to school with a pungent-footed guest licking my ear from the passenger seat. Alice gathered her school stuff and opened the back door.

"I think we should call her Macy," she pronounced.

"I think we should call her Temporary," I countered. Our dog at the time, Polly, was quite literally a cranky bitch of a certain age who viewed any attempt to interact with her as a gross invasion of privacy. We were going to remain a one-dog family.

That afternoon, I took Temporary Macy to our local animal hospital. She had no identifying chip. I checked the neighborhood where we found her. There were no "missing dog" signs taped to the telephone poles so I put up a dozen "found dog" signs and checked her into a nearby kennel. I boarded her for a week, visiting every day for pats and a walk, but no one responded to my signs. This was not entirely surprising as Temporary Macy was a mix of a couple of breeds frequently bred for urban protection or fighting; if they don't show promise, they're thrown away like old munitions. Actually, my affectionate ward was lucky, as many of her not-aggressive siblings are tormented to make them more vicious or, failing that, used for bait.

When I would visit her at the kennel, Temporary Macy would greet me with the kind of adoration reserved for those who have taken a bullet for the Pope. The kennel workers grew so fond of her they let her sleep under their feet while they worked the desk. It was abundantly clear she was domesticated, warmly social, and in crying need of a home. After a week passed, I decided to find her one. I knew it was time because finding her a home was the right thing to do and also because her kennel bill was beginning to wander up into weekend-escape-at-the-Ritz-Carlton territory.

I have never written a personal ad, but I cannot imagine making any greater effort to present someone in a more favorable light. I used phrases like "good listener," "attractive," "easy to please," and "mellow." I didn't mention how she likes long walks on the beach, picnics in front of a roaring fire, and exotic out-of-the-way restaurants, nor did I take off ten pounds or puff up her academic credentials, but I think I hit every other cliché of the genre. I did say she was "submissive" and "easy to control," which I suspect are familiar to readers of a different type of personal ad.

Within a few days, I had the good fortune to find her a home with friends of ours. Their son Dennis was slightly timid when it came to canine companionship but they felt such a mellow dog would be a natural introduction. The parents had never owned dogs before but Temporary Macy was so cheerful and easygoing, how hard could it be?

I wasn't promising them something just to get the dog off my hands. She was an eight-month-old sweetheart who seemed to need very little in the way of exercise beyond a walk a day. She was housebroken, quiet, and lived to sleep with her head on your feet. I didn't quite understand how a dog with at least two breeds in her that are known for energy and endurance was such a couch potato, but who was I to question the way of the dog? They named her Ursula, for her bear-like qualities. I considered the matter closed.

Three days later, I got the first phone call.

"Quinn," my friend began hesitantly. "Ursula ate a potato chip and now she's coughing."

"She might have scratched her throat. She's a tough puppy. She'll be better by tomorrow," I said reassuringly.

Two days later: "She seems to be happy and very active, but she's still coughing."

"She might have gotten kennel cough," I said, slightly less confidently. "If it doesn't clear up by tomorrow, take her to see the vet."

The next day she was drooling bile, coughing, and unable to stand. They raced her to the vet to learn that their new family member had something like pneumonia, only nastier. The next week for them was a blur of multiple medications crammed down Ursula's throat by plastic syringe, mopping pools of bile from the floor, and explaining to Dennis that if the dog fell down and didn't get back up, to come find Mommy and Daddy right away. Imagine *Lassie* meets *ER*, with a little *Exorcist* thrown in for texture.

And who was responsible for this blameless family going through such an awful experience? That would be me. I spent a lot of time on the phone saying things like, "I am so sorry . . . I just didn't know . . . You have to get up to medicate how often? Oh, God. I am so sorry."

A week passed, and then two. Slowly, Ursula got better. My friend was able to throw away the syringes. Ursula improved. She became healthy. She went beyond healthy into radiant, then energetic, then positively robust. We discovered a new layer to Ursula. What we had taken to be a mellow disposition was, in retrospect, the first symptoms of a life-threatening illness.

Healthy Ursula had enough energy to pull a Humvee full of cinderblocks up Pikes Peak. Healthy Ursula thought the proper way to greet people was to jump on them, knock them down, and stand on their sternum. Healthy Ursula ate shoes. Also doors. Healthy Ursula was a pet I *never* would have placed with a family looking for their first dog.

A month passed, and then another. I would hear stories from Ursula's family and they weren't great. These kind people had neither the time nor experience to be consistent and firm owners, which is the only way you can train an exuberant and willful puppy. She was getting stronger. The family was weakening. Unless Ursula could help out with mortgage payments, something had to give.

Saturday morning, I got a call. My friend was in tears.

"We just can't do it," she wailed. "She's the sweetest girl in the world, but I'm down to one pair of work shoes. She just won't stop and she won't listen. Would you please take her back?"

I looked around at Polly, my sullen elderly dog, at Lulabelle, my aggressively dog-loathing cat, and my child who doesn't especially like being licked or knocked over.

"Sure," I said with something that sounded almost like enthusiasm.

My job as Ursula's rescuer had just entered its you-rescue-it, you-own-it phase. Without proper and consistent training, Ursula would be bounced from house to house, getting weirder and wilder with each stay. She could end up in a shelter. In Los Angeles County, twenty-four hours after an "owner turn-in," a dog of her breed is destroyed. The only way I was going to save her sweet bouncy hide was by becoming the toughest alpha bitch in this area code.

Luckily, this comes naturally to me, which is odd because I have a cellular loathing of conflict and a hair-trigger reflex to be helpful—two characteristics rarely associated with strong leaders. As I understand it, Napoleon seldom offered to water people's plants when they were out of town. Still, if being obstinate means saving a life, I can put my niceness in storage with the winter gloves and old tax returns and get down to business. Which is why, on an overcast and colorless Monday afternoon, I walked through their front yard, past the Ursula-sized holes dug into the lawn, past the macerated garden gnome and the odd designer-shoe carcass to play full-throttle, one-on-one, *who's-your-bitch* with Ursula. The front door opened and Ursula, having seen me through the window, leapt in joyful greeting, aiming straight for my collarbone. I took her leash quickly, snapped it sharply, and barked, "SIT!"

The nose muzzle on her training leash did its job. Ursula froze for an instant, blinked in confusion, then rose back up on her hind legs and attempted to lead me in a waltz.

"SIT!" This time even sharper and meaner.

Again, she froze. I pressed her backside down. She sat.

I sang out merrily, "Good sit!" My voice had shifted from a sadistic Marine drill instructor to Glinda, the Good Witch of the North. Hearing a sweet tone, Ursula made for my shoulders again.

"SIT!" I pressed her backside down. She sat.

"Good sit!"

The rapid-fire toggle between my tone before the sit (*Full Metal Jacket*) and after the sit (*Mister Rogers' Neighborhood*) would have alarmed any reasonably alert psychologist. As it was, we hadn't even left the front porch and this sweet overgrown puppy was already bewildered. We said a quick good-bye to her old family, who shut the door behind us with the speed and resolve of prison guards. Ursula looked up at me with something approaching hope.

"Come, Ursula."

She leapt like Pegasus toward the front gate. I grabbed her by the collar.

"SIT!"

We composed ourselves.

"Come, Ur . . . SIT!"

I grabbed her by the muzzle, looked deeply into her eyes, and growled sharply. I don't suggest this was to be my Christmas card image, but it worked. She sat stock still, whining softly in confusion. This was nowhere near as much fun as chewing shoes.

After a moment to demonstrate the depth and breadth of my authority, we started off again, Ursula walking meekly beside me. We made it all the way to their gate—a distance of about five yards—when it occurred to Ursula: *Why, if I could just take this unspeakable thing off my snout, I could run as I please and show the world what a well-muscled dog with bad manners can really do!* She flung herself against the gate, attempting to work the muzzle off by rubbing her nose against the hinge. I grabbed her by the collar in an attempt to get her forelegs up.

"SIT!"

Seen from the outside, I'm sure it appeared I was trying to lynch her. I finally got her back into sit and while she pouted, I plotted. A full "heel" position (dog's right shoulder at your left hip, keeping pace with you while walking) might be more than she was capable of on her first walk. I decided to go for "walk," which would be dog at my left side, slightly behind me, on a loose leash. This was all theoretical, as "heel" and "walk" both imply traveling more than seven inches forward at any one time.

Meanwhile, the El Greco clouds, until then patchy and benign, thickened noiselessly overhead.

"Ursula, WALK!"

We stepped out of the gate. Ursula leapt ahead of me, as expected. What I did next must have entertained anyone who happened to look out their window.

You can't leash train a dog by dragging it by the collar because all you teach the dog is that this particular human has this weird fondness for randomly compressing its trachea. You have two choices. You can stop walking entirely until they happen to look up at you, to see if you died, and then start the walk again at your pace; or, you can walk quickly in a circle, using their forward momentum to neatly place them behind you.

So, I walked in a circle. Ursula ended up at my left side, a couple of inches behind me.

"Ursula, WALK!"

I began to notice how my dog-encouraging voice sounds uncannily like Mary Poppins. Ursula took two steps in the correct position. Then she saw a leaf and hurtled forward.

"SIT!"

She was now officially miserable. Inconsistent-yet-fun parents were becoming a distant memory. In this new life, she was somehow attached to Evil Psycho Stepmother. She lay down and sighed, nose between her paws. A fat drop of rain hit the ground an inch away. I tugged her back into a sitting position.

"Ursula, WALK!"

We almost made it to the next house this time before a raindrop on her back caused her to lose focus. We trudged in another tight circle and reestablished equilibrium.

We got another five feet before she decided to make a break for it, just for old times' sake.

"SIT!"

The good news was that she was sitting without my having to push her back down anymore. The bad news was that she wouldn't put her butt all the way on the wet ground, so it was less "sit," more "hover." I decided to accept it on technical points.

"Ursula, WALK!"

Ursula leapt away from the wet ground in relief, aiming to lick my jugular.

"SIT!"

She sat, her whole body language radiating misery. I looked at her in sympathy. All this shouting and circle-walking was in order to save her life, but she didn't know that. In this game, both the saviors and the saved lead lonely lives. It was raining steadily now and I leaned over and rubbed her ear.

She took this as a sign that this obeying silliness was over and that we could be ballroom dancing partners again.

"SIT!"

The very instant after I yelled, there was a rumble of thunder so deep and resonant I felt it in my spine. The dog stayed in sit, but stared up at the sky in absolute terror. I was yelling at her and God was yelling at her. This was by definition a bad-dog day. We squelched onward. Either she was finally learning the basic rules of "walk" or the by-now torrential rain sapped her of her fight. It was certainly draining away mine. I have new respect for anyone who trains dogs in Scotland.

Ursula and I walked two whole blocks this way. It took an hour and a half. I popped her into my car where I spent another twenty minutes convincing her that I didn't want her to drive, thank you. Then I brought her home, enjoying the last few minutes of quiet before not one single living thing in my house was happy.

After her march of misery, crossing the threshold of our back door cheered Ursula up tremendously. For one thing, the sky wasn't yelling at her anymore. For another, I hadn't yelled at her since the sidewalk. But best of all, there—in the corner of the dining room—was another dog. Ursula *loved* other dogs. At the inconsistent-but-fun domicile she'd just left, she had a best friend in the adjacent yard: a year-old golden retriever with whom she would spend hours on end alternately chasing, barking, and chewing each other's legs—not what I look for in a friendship, but I'm sure Ursula didn't want to get a pedicure and speculate about the hidden flaws of famous people, so we're even.

When Ursula spotted Polly, she saw something like a life jacket in a fur coat. *So what if the humans seem to be trying to deprogram me from a cult*, she thought. *I've got a dog buddy here and it'll be all chasing, barking, leg-chewing heaven from now on!* In a single leap, she crossed the room, landed next to Polly's bed, stuck her butt in the air, and barked excitedly. Polly opened one eye and scowled. Something had dared awaken her from one of her more critical afternoon naps.

Ursula waited a beat for our dog to take off from her bed and sprint around the room. When this didn't happen, she barked louder.

Polly curled one-third of her upper lip and growled warningly.

Ursula dropped to the ground in a submissive pose and wagged her tail furiously. She continued to bark in joyous abandon.

Polly took this as an invitation to flatten her ears against her head and growl an even more threatening growl than before, if such a noise were possible. Polly was really old, but arthritic hips and a weak bladder didn't shake her resolve to throw down with loud strangers with boundary issues.

I didn't think they'd end up as workout buddies, but I was hoping Ursula's joie de vivre might endear her to Polly. But no, it now looked as if Queen Victoria was being forced to share a dorm room with a Teletubby.

When I took Alice to school the next morning, I popped Ursula into the car with us. I assumed Polly needed some quality time alone.

On the way home, I stopped in Griffith Park and took Ursula for a long hike, which she enjoyed immeasurably. I enjoyed it too. It was a refreshing change to have a canine hiking buddy who didn't seek refuge under the first bush and refuse to take another step. Then I ran some errands, keeping Ursula in the car as needed, taking her with me when I could. I thought to myself, *I could do this. I could have a second dog that stays with me all day*. She's unbelievably sweet. I'll exercise and socialize her and Polly will have hours at home by herself when she can pretend Ursula is nothing more than a horrible dream. I do wish she'd stop licking my ear when we're on the freeway, though.

Heading to pick up Alice, we made a detour for groceries and I grabbed a takeout lunch that Ursula and I could share at an outside table. At the checkout, I ran into the mother of one of Alice's schoolmates, Emily. I gave her the short version of Ursula's wild ride.

"I'd love a third dog," she said enthusiastically. "My fourteen-year-old son has been begging for a dog of his own."

Hmm, this might work. They have dog experience. They have an energetic teenage boy, tall enough to tolerate full-body slams from a good-sized pet. They have developed a tolerance to dog hair on their clothing. Hmmm. I went to the car and brought out Ursula. She lay down on the sidewalk next to Emily's mom and gazed up through her long black lashes with moist adoration. The woman fairly swooned. I was most forthcoming about Ursula's charms and peculiarities, but I'm not sure how much she heard because Ursula was actively campaigning for the title of Most Precious Dog West of the Rockies. The love was fairly oozing in both directions.

Finally, she looked at her watch and said reluctantly, "I've got to do a couple more things before I pick up Emily. I'm going to think about this and talk to my husband. There's no point in talking to my son, he'll say it's a great idea."

"Okay," I said. "See you at school."

"Do me a favor," she said. "If Emily sees Ursula, don't tell her I'm even thinking about this. She's going to love this dog, and I need to make up my mind without that pressure."

When it came time to pick up Alice at school, I walked Ursula onto the outer playground. One fifth grader looked over and shrieked in delight, "DOG!"

Within thirty seconds, Ursula was swarmed by fifteen small, gleeful playmates. I'd never have done this without absolute confidence in Ursula's good nature, but she was even better than I hoped. She lay down on the ground, accepted all petting with pleasure, and licked whatever child body parts were near her tongue. I noticed Emily was one of the first kids to cuddle Ursula and one of the last to be peeled off when it came time for us to leave.

That night, I was making dinner when the phone rang. It was Emily's mother.

"I can't get Ursula out of my head," she said. "And Emily came home raving about her without even knowing I was thinking about this. My husband thinks I'm insane, but Emily and I want the dog."

I was delighted but cautious.

"Maybe we should have a playdate with Ursula and your dogs first?"

"No. We want her."

"Okay, do you want to stop by this weekend?"

"Actually, we were thinking tonight, so that my son could have her right away. Could we come by in about an hour?"

It couldn't be that easy?

"Uh, okay. I mean, yeah. Great! I'll have her stuff ready to go. We even have a crate for her, and we'll see you in about an hour."

I hung up the phone and saw Alice standing in the doorway, frowning.

"Who's coming over tonight?"

I said brightly, "Emily's mom has decided that Ursula would be a great addition to their family, and they're going to adopt her!"

It's amazing how I thought presenting this headline in my best good-news voice would negate what I was actually telling her. Alice's face crumpled.

"But . . . But, I wanted her to sleep on my bed."

I swung quickly into, "I know it's hard to give up a sweet dog like Ursula, but every quadruped in the house hates her . . . Her new family goes for lots of walks and has another dog that is closer in age to Ursula . . . And she'll be with someone we know again, so we can visit her . . . A lot!"

I might as well have acted out the Mahabharata with spoons for all the good it did. Alice flung herself into her room, sobbing, and slammed the door. I followed her to the threshold.

"Do you want me to come in?"

"No. I want to cry!"

I tried saying supportive things through the door like, "I hear that you're upset." The parenting magazines suggest reflecting what the child is feeling back to them.

"JUST STOP TALKING!" she shouted, between sobs.

The parenting magazines have never provided me with a single relevant parenting tip. At this point, all I could think was, *if Alice and I had been driving down that street just five minutes later, I might have a peaceful house right now.* Then again, you never know. We're an emotional people.

Emily and her mother arrived at seven on the dot. I liberated Ursula from her crate and she ran joyfully to them. Alice hid in the corner of the living room and sniffed. She didn't want to be part of the good-bye, but she wasn't going to miss seeing it. When Emily, her mother, and Ursula left, Alice collapsed in my lap and cried while I stroked her hair.

A week later, the woman who adopted Ursula sought me out
at school. Turns out, their dog, who was supposed to be thrilled
to have a new canine companion, didn't feel quite up to having
a roommate who wanted to play incessantly and sleep sprawled
across his skull. After a week of threats and feints, the two dogs
had come to blows over a bone, and Ursula's third loving mother
in three months realized it was never going to work.

Ursula arrived back at my house with her crate, three new
chew toys, a huge bag of food, and the pleasant expression of
someone who no longer attempts to understand what's going
on. I, however, knew exactly what was going on. I had signed on
for a dog-life's worth of the kind of close monitoring not seen in
public since *One Flew Over the Cuckoo's Nest*.

I took Ursula everywhere, which usually ended with me
apologizing. She went to the grocery store with me one morning
and while waiting outside, entertained herself by chewing the
wheels off a grocery cart. Any meal I ate at a restaurant was
taken al fresco so Ursula could lick my toes and knock over the
table when a potential play mutt appeared anywhere in a two-
hundred-yard radius. At home, I even took her into the bathroom with me, reasoning that whatever performance anxiety a
fifty-pound dog crawling into your lap might create, it was less
stressful than flying out of the bathroom, pulling your pants up
from around your ankles while trying to remove your cat's head
from your houseguest's maw.

I stopped thinking in terms of *When I find her the right
home . . .* My mind was filled with more practical musings such
as, *Put Ursula in her crate so Lulabelle can come in and eat her
dinner. Then put Lulabelle in the kid's room, put Ursula in the
back yard, and feed Polly her dinner. Walk Ursula. Then let Ur-*

sula have her dinner while I walk Polly. My life started to re-semble the riddle about the farmer, the fox, the chicken, and the rowboat. I always hated that riddle.

Sometimes, when popping Ursula into the car for a trip to the drive-through ATM, the drive-through pharmacy, and whatever vegetarian lunch I could grab at a drive-through, I would stare at her and wonder if this could have been avoided. What if I had left her on the street? But that was never going to happen because I'm one of the good guys. I might not be having much fun right now and my hair might smell of dog saliva, but this dog was better off because of me.

One afternoon, I crated Ursula in anticipation of taking Polly for her midday walk. Polly walked by Ursula's crate and threw a quick "Yeah! Mommy loves ME!" sneer in Ursula's di-rection. Ursula sighed deeply, put her big head on her paws, and looked doleful. I had a flash of inspiration. I'd let her stay in the back yard while I walked Polly, after which I would walk Ur-sula. It was a lovely day and the squirrels were looking espe-cially plump and disrespectful. Within minutes, Polly and I were on our way and Ursula was standing under the squirrel tree, looking up and grinning wildly.

Polly and I walked around the block. As we returned toward the house I noticed a van stopped in the middle of the street and two men talking on the sidewalk. One of them, relating an anecdote, clapped his hands together sharply once, then pointed up the street, away from our house. Turning back, they noticed me.

"Hey," the hand clapper called, "is this your house?"

He pointed to our yard.

"Yeah?" I said, acid flooding my stomach.

"Do you have a yellow dog?"

"No," I said shakily. "I have a brown dog." Because that's what I do in moments of terror, I try to get out of things on a technicality.

"About that big?" he asked, putting his hand just about Ursula-height. I nodded dumbly. He sighed.

"I was just driving along here, and it jumped that wall and ran out in front of me. I tried to stop but it bounced off the front of my van," and he clapped his hands together, "and ran off that way." He pointed up the street. The driver was a big man with a tattoo snaking up from his shirt collar. He took a ragged breath and said, "I couldn't stop fast enough. I tried. I really love dogs. It was just . . ." and he clapped his hands together again. His hands were large. The sound seemed to echo down the empty block.

I bolted into the yard, hoping that somehow another brown/yellow dog about Ursula's height had run through our yard, scaled the fence, and gotten hit, leaving my charming ninny standing under the squirrel tree, but the yard was empty. I put Polly inside, carefully not looking at Ursula's empty crate, grabbed her leash, and dashed back outside. For an hour, I walked the neighborhood, shouting her name and sobbing. I had broken my promise to keep her safe, and I couldn't have been in any more pain if I had broken my arm. No one on the street had seen her. No one in the neighboring streets had seen her. In the days to come, no one responded to my signs. She had vanished as abruptly as she arrived.

Before we head down a particularly shadowy and unpleasant road, let me stop right here and introduce a psychiatric term: "compartmentalization." For those of you who don't freely toss this word around when ordering a Frappuccino, here's a brief definition: "Compartmentalization is the psychological ability to assign thoughts, beliefs, or life experiences into separate categories in your brain." At its best, this means you can have a complete knock-down drag-out with your boyfriend over breakfast—one of those verbal brawls that ends in the phrase "Maybe we should see other people!"—and still manage a productive day at work. A compartmentalized brain would file the screaming domestic argument under "Home," and because "Home" has nothing to do with "Work," you can function at the office—that is until the day you find yourself screaming into the work phone over the custodial arrangements of copper cookware and your joint collection of snow globes.

That's compartmentalization at its best. At its worst, you are me and for two weeks after the accident you've been worrying about Ursula's welfare while at least once a day you've also found yourself thinking, *What is that odd smell in the front yard? Must be a skunk.* Because that's what skunks do, they smell like death all the time, right? If you compartmentalize well enough you never, not even once, not even in the darkest most pessimistic recesses of your brain, wonder if the smell of death and the absent dog might possibly maybe somehow be related. It took Consort and his somber lucidity to bring things to a close.

One morning, I stumbled out of bed and headed for the front door to grab the paper. When I opened the front door there was Consort in his grubby crawling-under-the-house gear. I blinked in trepidation. For the first half hour of the day I fear any change in routine, and finding Consort up before me qualified as a shift in the universe akin to Oprah driving NASCAR.

He stood in the doorway, brushing dirt off his pants. He breathed in, looked at me, and said kindly, "I found Ursula."

One of the weaknesses of compartmentalization is that the walls between the things the compartmentalizer knows are tall, but fragile. All it takes is the tiniest puff to bring them down. In a second, I knew he hadn't found her alive. I knew she had been in the front yard. It had been weeks since she was last seen. I cried in sorrow and also in horror of what he must have found.

He held me close and said, "I think she swung around and came back right after the accident the first day. She was way under the outer hedge, which is why we didn't see her. I had a hunch, so I went looking."

I asked him, "Was she in pain when she died?" knowing full well he had no idea but pathetically prepared to accept any palliative he was willing to offer. He shook his head firmly and said, "I think her injuries were bad enough so she just lay down and went to sleep. I wrapped her up and put her in the dog run."

I cried again, filled with guilt over what Consort must have seen and handled, and what Ursula had suffered. I had driven to shelters twenty miles away to check on whether she had been picked up, and she had been a few steps from my front door. If I had only looked . . .

Mostly, I grieved for having broken my word. I like being the grown-up. I am of service. I help. But this time I brought the dog in from a near-certain death on a busy boulevard to have her die on a quiet street, yards away from the person who vowed to take care of her. In my successful moments, when my altruism works out, I bask in the light of being the good guy. The dark side of being the good guy is the moment where you don't solve the problem, and someone ends up saying, "You

tried your best." That seems like a fairly obvious statement because the whole point of being an honorable person is that you
try your best; if it doesn't work, well, no one's expecting perfection. So why was the idea that I did my best for Ursula breaking
my heart?

Because once again my best had been pretty damn pathetic.
The dog had died because I didn't understand exactly how
much she loved me, how desperate she was to be with me all the
time. How high she could jump. I made a stupid mistake and an
innocent creature was dead. And the man I loved had been
forced to attend to the consequences. I saw a lifetime ahead of
me of trying my best and seeing how small and pitiful my best
really was. I sobbed again. And then I dried my tears and woke
up Alice. It is a measure of age appropriate self-absorption and
an inclination toward ignoring the anomalous before 9:00 a.m.
that my daughter noticed nothing. I got her to school and then I
called the pet crematorium. They were polite and respectful;
they'd pick her up that day and cremate her for me.

"Do you want Ursula back afterward?" the woman asked.

"Yes," I said hollowly. "We'll bury her at home."

I put her ashes next to the hedge where she had been found,
because she had come home. For a stray found trotting down
a street, Ursula, in her last moments, knew where to go. She had
a home. And that was all I had to console me. I had given her a
few months of love, a fair amount of yelling, and a working
knowledge of the words "sit," "heel," and "stop, you idiot!"
I had scratched her back. I had saved her from an immediate
death even if I couldn't save her from her fate. I found her a loving home. Three times. I had taken her on hikes. Dozens of kids
had petted her. I fed her the expensive stuff and a few french

fries. I knew exactly who Ursula was capable of becoming and I loved her anyway. During my watch, any hand that touched her did so with kindness. My madcap foster child was a world-class chore, but during the entire time I knew her she never once looked up at me without an ear-to-ear grin. I did the best I could. What else is there?

It's the Pictures That Got Small

ONE MORNING, AFTER HEARING HOW MY CALL WAS VERY important to them, how calls were being taken in the order received, and humming along to something that sounded like "I Could Have Danced All Night" played by an orchestra of nose-harpists, I was finally rewarded with a living human being. I could now order checks.

To access my account, I had to give this human being every relevant detail of my personal life. Distinguishing moles? Check. Dental records? Check. Contents of my glove compartment including the serial number on the tin of Sucrets? Check. As I was spelling my name for the third time, she suddenly piped up, "Oh, you have a famous name."

I could have argued it is more accurately described as a-name-known-by-a-few-people-with-a-passion-for-trivia-and-members-of-my-daughter's-carpool, but since I couldn't think of anything better, I responded with the simple yet always useful, "Huh."

I heard a few more seconds of typing and then, "I wonder what ever happened to her."

I toyed with telling her I'd heard Quinn Cummings died at the hands of her pimp.

I toyed with insisting I was quite certain no one else had my name and then throwing a fit if she mentioned the words "former child actor."

I toyed with speculating that Quinn Cummings has made millions from bank fraud, specializing in counterfeit checks.

Instead, I said, honestly, "Oh, probably a bunch of stuff" and listened to her type and chuckle at the thought of the wild life that the other Quinn Cummings must be living.